SEX HAPPENS

SEX HAPPENS

The Gay Man's Guide to
Creative Intimacy

ARLEN KEITH LEIGHT, Ph.D.

Langdon Street Press
322 First Avenue N, 5th floor
Minneapolis, MN 55401
612.455.2293
www.langdonstreetpress.com

Edited by Robert Schmidt
Cover design by Daniel Wasinger
Internal design and layout by Burton & Associates
Distributed by Itasca Books
The illustration in Appendix Four is used with permission from
    Aaron Silverman of SCB Distributors.

ISBN-13: 978-1-62652-384-5
ISBN-10: 2013949919

Book Website:
    MarriageCounselingForMen.org/SexHappens
Email:
    DrLeight@MarriageCounselingForMen.org

Throughout *Sex Happens* the author has changed or avoided using names, altered
circumstances, and created composites of actual situations to protect personal identity and
confidentiality while maintaining the integrity of the exemplary scenarios to provide the
reader with true-to-life insight.

Printed in the United States of America.

IN MEMORY OF CHARLES

who continues to teach me that
authentic love is unconditional,
transcends the ego's need to be right,
survives the greatest of life's challenges,
and
lasts forever.

Contents

Acknowledgments ix

Introduction xi
*Be Honest with Yourself and Be Honest with
Your Partner*

PART ONE
Consciousness and Communication: The Fundamental Components of Creative Intimacy

Chapter One 3
*Man-to-Man Relationships: Unique Challenges and
Obstacles to Intimacy*

Chapter Two 23
*Where Did the Passion Go? How Sexual Intimacy
Evolves or Dissolves*

Chapter Three 41
*Creative Intimacy through Dialogue: Exercises for
Expansive Communication of Feelings and Emotions*

PART TWO
Creative Sexual Enhancement

Chapter Four 81
Sexual Desire vs. Sexual Disorder

Chapter Five 91
*The Sensual Journey: Seven Exercises for
Creative Intimacy*

Chapter Six 133
Creative Intimacy: Fun, Frolic and Fantasy

PART THREE
Creative Relationship Re-Contracting

Chapter Seven 157
Relationship Paradigms and Contracts:
Creative Intimacy and Permission to Choose

Chapter Eight 177
Developing Your Creative Relationship Agreement

Chapter Nine 211
Relationship Sabbatical: A Creative Solution for
Mending or Ending

Afterword. 227

Appendix One 229
Evolution of a Relationship

Appendix Two 231
Inventory of Feelings

Appendix Three 235
Dialogue Analysis from Chapter Three

Appendix Four 243
Effects of Angle of Entry on Rectal Insertion

Appendix Five 245
Example Relationship Agreement

Appendix Six. 249
Example Addendum to the Relationship Agreement

Appendix Seven 251
Example Sabbatical Agreement

References 255

Index 261

Acknowledgments

I am so grateful to the many individuals who played a role in the writing of this book.

When I was in social work school, my mentor and supervisor Professor Elizabeth Smith, DSW, was the first to help me understand the importance of the relationship between intimacy and vulnerability. In my PhD sexology program, Professor William Granzig, PhD, contributed to my deeper understanding of sex and sexual intimacy in loving relationships and in life. I am most appreciative of the role all my teachers played in my graduate education, with special commendation to Drs. Smith and Granzig.

Through the process of writing this book, Marilyn K. Volker, EdD, renowned sexologist, reviewed my work chapter by chapter. Dr. Volker was instrumental in assuring validity and accuracy while giving alternative opinions and suggestions. I could not have made this book happen without Dr. Volker's advice and direction. I am very, very grateful for her guidance.

Additionally, Rick Koonce, life coach and writer, guided my writing for style as well as content. I very much appreciate his time and perceptive personal and professional perspective.

I would also like to thank my colleagues and friends George Kallas, PsyD, Norman Abramson, MD, Jerry

Glatzer, DDS, and Robert T. Versteeg, MSW, as well as my sister, Giselle H. Light, MA, SLP, for their review, critique, and suggestions.

I am deeply indebted to all of the clients who have allowed me the honor and privilege to counsel them, as well as those men with whom I have had intimate connections. They have been, in many ways, my most valuable teachers.

And, finally, I would like to thank my parents for modeling a truly loving, intimate relationship and providing me the foundation for creating an authentically lived and fulfilling life.

Introduction

"Be Honest with Yourself and Be Honest with Your Partner"

My father died a decade ago. Before receiving his diagnosis of pancreatic cancer, Dad had been a vibrantly healthy man. He took exceptional care of himself, and he took immense pride in his body. A weightlifter since adolescence, he continued pumping iron and riding his bike up to 100 miles almost every weekend at the age of sixty-nine. He was still running the business he started in his forties, designing and manufacturing diagnostic medical equipment. Dad was quite the well-rounded man: an athlete, an intellectual, highly educated, professionally successful, and—most important to him—a family man who cherished his wife and children. He would always greet me with a hug and a kiss, never concerned about putting on some macho façade because I am another man or because I happen to be gay. He embraced me, my life and my life partner. He was my support, my advisor and my confidante. He always seemed to have "the answer." He loved life, and before he ever had a chance to retire, he was stricken with that most deadly and devastating cancer. He lived eight months of hell watching his well-cared-for physique and his vision of traveling the world with his wife of forty-eight years deteriorate before his eyes.

Not long after his death, my mother and I had the grim task of going through his belongings clearing the way for a life without dad's physical presence. I took it upon myself to go through the more personal items in his nightstand and medicine cabinet. His electric razor, toothbrush, comb, cologne and deodorant all evoked memories of this man I loved dearly. Then there were the medications. Pain pills, vitamins, herbs, Viagra, more pain pills...Viagra? I looked at the label on the medicine bottle and, indeed, it was Viagra that had been prescribed by his oncologist! Dad was still having sex, or at least trying to, even after starting chemotherapy for cancer. (If you don't know, pancreatic cancer is a horrific disease because it is usually diagnosed in the late stages of its progression. Dad had thirteen "spots" on his liver at the time of diagnosis, meaning it had spread extensively. The treatment is extremely aggressive, despite its lack of long-term success, and patients often find themselves in tremendous pain, devastatingly weak, and filled with abdominal fluid.) Despite the pain, the weakness, and the despair, my father wanted to continue to make love to my mother.

My parents had always been a very physical and sensual couple. My father would often caress my mother's shoulders or waist, hold her hand or give her a kiss. When I was a child, I recall waking up at night and going down into our den to find my parents romantically dancing to soft music. I remember going into their bedroom on weekend mornings when my father and mother would stay in bed late. I asked my father what the blue package and balloon were on his nightstand. Dad said it was a special kind of bandage. And there was the time I went to the kitchen midday to get a snack to find my father sensuously reaching for my mom's behind.

I found myself struck by the fact that not only were my parents still having an active sex life into their late sixties after forty-eight years of marriage, but they were fooling around while my father was depressed, in pain, weak and dying of cancer. I loved the realization of my discovery, but I found myself feeling sad and filled with grief. To be sure, part of my personal pain was because of the loss of my dad and all he meant to my mom and me. But, I also recognized how, at age forty-four, my own sex life with my partner of nineteen years had ended years before, and I had done virtually nothing to re-create physical intimacy in my relationship. I knew this wasn't about living up to some standard based on my parents' relationship, but I realized more than ever that I had been in a relationship that was sexually less than satisfactory for me. On the other hand, I loved my partner, and he was my best friend. The ambivalence I was feeling about my relationship came to a head with my father's untimely death. I found myself thinking "Okay, so I'm not going to live forever. How many more years do I want to go on without a sex life?" Clearly, it was time to end the silence around the issue of sex. I went into therapy with my partner.

After interviewing several psychotherapists, we agreed on someone we felt had a solid approach and would be even-handed. He was excellent with his base of knowledge and expertise, and my partner and I finally dialogued about the difficult issues we had avoided for years. After eleven grueling months of spilling our guts out to one another, we were no closer to having sex than we were when we began therapy. I felt that I had to make a decision about whether to continue to be in a relationship that was filled with love and trust, or leave because we were more like brothers than lovers. I felt I had nowhere to turn for an answer. I was wishing my father were around to give me advice.

It was a cold, gloomy, drizzly November day in Washington, DC. I decided to take the forty-five minute drive out to the suburban cemetery where we had buried my father fifteen months earlier. I sat on the damp ground at his grave and cried. I was in such turmoil and pain. I loved my partner. We essentially had grown up together. I couldn't imagine my life without him. But I did not want to continue to live without some sort of sexual connection, preferably sexual intimacy. I felt as though I was living with one foot out the door, and that didn't seem fair to me or my partner. I couldn't bear the thought of hurting the man I loved, but wasn't I hurting him by staying with him while wanting to be somewhere else or with someone else? Our relationship had been monogamous, which essentially meant celibate. There was no one else in my life, but there was this nagging thought in my mind that there might be the potential for passionate sexual intimacy with someone else.

I closed my eyes, my face wet with tears and mist, and I asked my father what I should do. What came to me was his voice from beyond. The message rang true in my head and in my heart, and it was to be the basis of my life and my life's work. Dad answered, *"Be honest with yourself and be honest with your partner."* My heavy heart sobbed uncontrollably as I knew this was "the answer." I also knew this was much easier said than done. But, it is the message I pass on to you as you go through this book. Finding the honest answer inside your heart is often tougher than sharing it with your partner. However, *both* pieces are necessary for intimacy.

> *"Be honest with yourself and be honest with your partner."*

Sex is an important part of most men's lives. Sex can also be terribly confusing and evoke conflicting emotions. You probably picked up this book because some aspect of sexual intimacy in your life is in need of fulfillment or creative enhancement. Or perhaps you want to be sure future relationships will work to create loving intimacy and be sexually fulfilling and sustainable. This book cannot substitute for good work with a qualified sexologist or psychotherapist. My professional work since the visit to my father's grave site has been in the area of intimacy and sexology with gay men. The book you are about to read, based upon years of clinical and personal experience, is arranged in a deliberate order. The step-by-step format for the reader is the same journey I take couples on in private therapy when they are experiencing concerns with sex and intimacy. I encourage you not to jump forward in the book but, rather, to read it in sequence because the unfolding is a process that builds upon itself.

~

There is no work more vital for a loving relationship than honest dialogue.

~

There is no work more vital for a loving relationship than honest dialogue. As per my dad's advice, start by having an honest dialogue with yourself, and then engage your partner. This book will explain why you have the challenges you face, how to talk about them with your partner, how to create deepening levels of intimacy, how to re-engage your sexual connection, how to create a relationship contract around your sexual interests and desires, and how to create space should your relationship require a time-out. Nothing successful happens in relationships without good, solid, authentic communication.

The purpose of this book is to take you (and your partner) on a journey to experience love, intimacy and peace of mind. *Intimacy is a deep, loving connectedness that results from an opening of heart and soul.* This opening allows both partners to experience themselves and each other at their innermost cores in their most vulnerable places. *Everyone has a fear of intimacy*—true intimacy, that is. True intimacy requires looking deep into ourselves. And what could be more frightening than looking deep into ourselves? Only sharing our most vulnerable, fragile places with the ones we love.

~

Intimacy requires complete honesty and transparency with yourself and with your partner.

~

Intimacy requires complete honesty and transparency with yourself and with your partner. When there is true intimacy, there is no defensiveness, there is no judgment, there is no secrecy, there is no hiding, and there is no ego needing to be strong or autonomous. However, intimacy is not dependency. Intimacy is about accommodating and surrendering to another—not to placate or control, but to enhance your own experience in the relationship. *Intimacy is about coming to know yourself in a way that is only possible in the deepest connection with another, resulting in growth for both partners and for the relationship itself.*

Creative intimacy, the focus of this book, is the mutual opening of heart and soul—by design—to discover deeper levels of loving connectedness. Creative intimacy involves continuous self-discovery and self-acceptance, as well as sharing that deeper understanding and inspiration with our partner. *Creative intimacy requires honest disclosure and dialogue through innovative communication and physical exploration. While sex and intimacy are not identical, sensuality and sexuality both provide openings to our deepest, most vulnerable core selves.* Creative intimacy includes new solutions to dissolve barriers to both physical and emotional intimacy. Creative intimacy necessitates paradigm shifts for inventive re-contracting of a relationship on an ongoing basis. *Creative intimacy means maintaining a sense of authentic wholeness, while going deeper into vulnerable places with your partner.*

Creative intimacy is ultimately the exploration and the expression of your emotional needs and sexual desires in the context of your current authentic experience and feelings. This is achieved, first and foremost, through honest introspection, and then through open dialogue with your partner.

You may find some of your experiences are validated by the perspective I put forward. You may also find yourself seriously challenged and even angry or defensive reading some of the material in these pages. If (or when) some aspect of the book creates tension, anxiety or defensiveness in you, I ask you to consider the closely held belief(s) you may be hanging on to that could be limiting your vision or your potential. Sit for a while with the concept that is producing discomfort rather than dismissing it outright. Please note: I do not claim to have all the answers regarding gay sex and intimacy, but I do have an opinion and a perspective based upon my personal and professional experience. You do not have to agree, accept or buy into my approach or point of view. As Winston Churchill said, "People just disagree." Take from these pages what works for you and leave the rest behind. My intention is to stimulate your thinking, challenge your beliefs, and *give you permission to change your thinking and beliefs* within the context of

> *Creative intimacy is ultimately the exploration and the expression of your emotional needs and sexual desires in the context of your current authentic experience and feelings.*

the unique and respected perspective you bring to the material presented. I encourage you to make choices and changes based upon what feels right and works for you and your partner.

This book is written as a guide for:

1. Couples who are dissatisfied with the sexual connection they share

2. Couples who love each other but have lost passion or sexual desire for one another

3. Couples who have difficulty communicating effectively

4. Couples who are in conflict or near a crisis point

5. Couples who wish to explore new ways to create intimacy and connect physically with each other

6. Couples who wish to create an exclusive or open sexual relationship contract

7. Coupled men who are confused or ambivalent about staying in their relationships

8. Singles who want to improve their chances for creative intimacy and sustainable sexual passion in new love relationships

9. Singles who need some guidance for determining when a match is worth pursuing

10. Singles who wish to sidestep some of the pitfalls that create intimacy problems in long-term relationships

11. Professionals who work with gay men on sexual intimacy issues

You (and your partner) will want to commit to spending time, energy and effort working with the questions and exercises contained in this book. Don't rush your exploration. When I take couples in therapy through this work, it can take six weeks to six months—or longer. Allow the process to unfold at a slow but steady pace. Don't let the time commitment discourage you. *If you don't do it, tomorrow will be the same as today.*

Bring to this journey an open mind, an open heart and a willingness to expand your consciousness about the meaning and experience of intimacy. The result will be the creation of a deeper and more satisfying intimate connection with your partner.

(The descriptive definition of intimacy on page xv was quoted, compiled and adapted from *Intimacy: Trusting Oneself and the Other* by Osho and *The Art of Intimacy* by Thomas Patrick Malone.)

If you don't do it, tomorrow will be the same as today.

PART ONE

Consciousness and Communication: The Fundamental Components of Creative Intimacy

Chapter One

Man-to-Man Relationships: Unique Challenges and Obstacles to Intimacy

H ave you ever heard the statement "the only difference between gay people and straight people is that gay people are sexually attracted to the same sex and straight people are attracted to the opposite sex"? There is no more validity to that than the statement "the only difference between white people and black people is the color of their skin." These well-intentioned, but misleading, arguments are attempts to diminish the differences between groups of people and highlight the similarities. It can be argued that people of African descent have more in common with people of European descent than they have differences, but by reducing the difference to skin color, we devalue the biological, historical and cultural uniqueness of each race. Similarly, attempting to minimize the difference between homosexuals and heterosexuals devalues the important human variation and uniqueness of life experience of the individuals in these groups. We, therefore, can also conclude that the human experience for gay men is substantially different from that of straight men. And, of course, a man-to-man relationship is going to be substantially different from a man-to-woman relationship—as are its challenges.

This chapter offers insight into the *unique* challenges and obstacles to intimacy facing men in relationships with men. It is not intended to enumerate every relational difficulty, but rather to help the reader to understand significant difficulties gay men, in particular, confront as a critical baseline necessary for the pursuit of creative intimacy.

Challenge #1: Self-Acceptance

The world is changing and, with it, the traditional definition of family. There are an increasing number of countries—and states in the U.S.—that have legalized same-sex marriage, thereby creating a new national and international norm. This is a wonderful and necessary step in the process of reducing heterosexism worldwide. However, it cannot be denied that until there is universal acceptance of homosexuality as a normal human variance, we will all live under the cloud of homophobia and heterosexism. As defined by Jacobson and Gurman in the *Clinical Handbook of Couple Therapy:* "Homophobia is the fear and hatred of same-sex intimacy, love and sexuality and those individuals and institutions that are or are perceived to support, affirm or participate in such coupling. Heterosexism, on the other hand, is the privileging by the culture and its institutions of heterosexual forms of relating while simultaneously devaluing non-heterosexual forms of relating." Any restriction of marriage to male-female coupling is a clear example of a society's heterosexist orientation. A gay person growing up in such an environment receives the message that heterosexual relationships are legitimate and homosexual relationships are not. Even the most self-accepting, consciously affirming gay man is going to have internalized some of these cultural messages.

It is nearly impossible to grow up gay in America—or most anywhere in the world—without being adversely affected by societies that overtly and covertly instill the virtues of the heterosexual family and traditional marriage while devaluing and debasing the "homosexual lifestyle." All gay people function in the context of an oppressive social environment (some more than others, depending upon geographic location). The result is often an unconscious or semi-conscious sense that one's life and one's relationships are not as good as they could have been if one were straight. These feelings of being "less than" or even unworthiness are often manifest in an attempt to minimize the differences between ourselves and our straight counterparts either verbally or behaviorally. Marriage equality is unquestionably necessary in the struggle to end heterosexism. However, it can be argued that the legalization movement is driven, in part, by internalized heterosexist desires to minimize the differences between gay and straight relationships. Then the questions arise: "Can we honor our gay partnerships as inherently different from straight marriages?" and "Is the traditional marriage paradigm truly the best option for committed gay men?"

So, how do you have a fully satisfying, sexually intimate gay relationship when you feel it is not as good as, as valid as, or as legitimate as, the one your parents or other straight couples have? Well, you can't. While we work for equal rights, marriage equality and an end to heterosexism, we cannot ignore the need to engage the personal struggle to accept ourselves, our uniqueness, the uniqueness of our relationships and our feelings as homosexual men. *Full self-acceptance is an essential precursor for intimate partnering.*

Full self-acceptance is an essential precursor for intimate partnering.

Carl Jung, the renowned 20th-century Swiss psychiatrist, one of the fathers of modern-day psychology, coined some of the words we use in our current daily language. He spoke of the "persona" as the part of ourselves we show the world, and the "shadow" as the part we hide. We usually hide this side because of shame, because of a lack of confidence or because we simply don't like that part of ourselves. We imagine others would not like that side if they knew about it. Closeted gay men and women have their sexual orientation hidden in their shadow side. Indeed, most gay people have their gayness in the shadow at some time until coming out. Jung postulated that in order for us to live our lives fully we must embrace this shadow side. We don't have to like it, and we may even work to change some aspects of this shadow side (not sexual orientation), but we need to start with full self-acceptance.

Growing up in a society that devalues homosexuality, gay men often look outside of themselves for acceptance and validation. Gay subculture has taken the at-large cultural admiration of youth and beauty to new heights. This aggrandizement of the physical is, to some degree, a means for getting noticed and validated. Buying into cultural idealism is a sure prescription for diminishing one's sense of self. True self-worth and self-acceptance are independent of *external* validation. Embracing and accepting oneself completely comes from developing an *internal* sense of one's own good, worthiness and love. We cannot expect someone to accept us any more than we accept ourselves; and we cannot expect someone to love us any more than we love ourselves. Without mutual acceptance and love we cannot create a deeply intimate relationship.

Questions to Ponder:
(by yourself or with your partner)

1. What were the messages you received growing up—from family, religion, school, the government and the media—about being in a gay relationship? How do these messages affect your feelings about your relationship or gay relationships in general and their legitimacy today?

2. If there were a pill that would change your sexual orientation, honestly, would you swallow it? Do you and your partner feel the same way about this? How do your feelings about being gay affect your ability to connect with other gay men?

3. Have you ever entered into or stayed in a relationship just to prove to yourself or to others in your life that your relationships are as legitimate as heterosexual relationships? If you answered yes, what does that tell you about your feelings regarding gay relationships?

4. Do you embrace yourself fully and completely as a good, loving and worthy man? Do you look externally to others for self-acceptance and validation? Have you tried to live up to cultural standards of beauty only to feel worse about yourself? How do you think you might begin to look inward to find a loving sense of self?

Challenge #2: Gay Identity Development

The social pressures to conform to a heterosexual way of life and the lack of visible homosexual role models keep many gay men in the closet for years beyond the adolescent calling for sexual connection. As such, gay identity development does not parallel the heterosexual adolescent-to-adult developmental path. Some gay kids know and accept their sexual orientation from the time they are small children, while others come out at mid-life or later. Gay emotional, sexual and psychological adolescence, therefore, is often delayed beyond physical, biological and chronological adolescence. Another challenge to gay relationships, then, is age-independent development. Even partners who are chronologically the same age may be different developmentally with respect to self-acceptance as a gay person, experience with sex and intimacy, attitudes about being "out" in the world, and emotional maturity. Understanding these differences is of vital importance when gay couples deal with sexual issues.

Jack, 37, and Larry, 33, have been together for five years. When they met, Jack had been out for fifteen years, while Larry had only recently come out. They are very much in love, but Larry is wondering what he missed out on as a result of not having "sown his wild oats." The couple is experiencing difficulty, as Larry wants to explore his sexuality while Jack knows Larry is the only one he wants to be with intimately.

Mack, 29, and Dave, 30, have also been together for five years. Mack came out as a teenager and Dave only came out a year before the couple met and had dated only one other guy. The pair is experiencing substantial conflict relative to several issues, and their sexual connection has all but stopped. Mack wants out, but Dave is willing to do anything to save the relationship because he is afraid of going out into the "gay world."

These examples underscore the unpredictability of the impact of developmental difference on each unique couple. *Unpredictability is the nature of ALL relationships.* Gay relationships are often *more* unpredictable due to differences in maturation. Partners need to talk about these differences and how they impact the couple's intimate connection.

> *Unpredictability is the nature of ALL relationships.*

Questions to Ponder:

1. Is age difference an issue in your relationship? Is there a developmental difference that is independent of age? What conflicts or challenges are the results of a difference in age or age-independent development?

2. Is there anything you feel you've missed out on as a result of a delayed adolescence? How does that impact your relationship?

3. What do you imagine your life would look like now if you had been "out" from childhood? Do you feel delayed development has created any sense of loss, grieving or resentment that impacts your intimate relationships, sexually or otherwise?

Challenge #3: The Male Character, Temperament and Personality

In his best-selling book *Men Are From Mars, Women Are From Venus*, John Gray aptly describes the male-female dynamic that creates conflict and misunderstanding in heterosexual relationships. Gray explains how, at the end of a tough day, a wife comes home and relates to her husband how terrible she feels because of all the problems she faced at work. Her husband neglects the "feeling" part and begins to tell his wife how she can make things better at her job. He analyzes the situation and finds his solution to her problems so he can fix it and make it all better. His wife does not want his advice (at least not right away). She wants his love, compassion and empathy. She wants him to put his arms around her and say, "That sounds horrible. You must be feeling awful. Let's just sit down together for a while and chill out." In reality, *most everyone wants an empathic response before receiving advice.* Most women are expert at the warm-fuzzy stuff because they are socialized to express feelings first. Men are, more often than not, taught to hide their feelings. How often did we hear, growing up, "big boys don't cry"? So when men have a bad day, Gray explains, they go off into their caves. Their wives feel abandoned and left out, not being able to offer the love they want to give.

> *...most everyone wants an empathic response before receiving advice.*

When women get together, they most frequently talk about family, friends and relationships. When men get together they are likely to talk about work, sports and sex. One of my colleagues in Fort Lauderdale once said to me that the only thing gay men want to talk about there is sex and real estate. The difference in the way men and women generally deal with emotions is also reflected in how much men and women talk in any given day. It has been estimated that men use approximately 7,000 words per day whereas women speak 20,000. As such, the verbal areas of a woman's brain tend to be significantly more developed than a man's. Other studies show that estrogen, the "female" hormone, is a key auditory hormone. Additionally, men in most cultures are generally socialized to be independent and competitive; women are usually socialized to be inter-dependent and cooperative.

Okay, so now let's put two typical men together in an intimate relationship and see what we get. They *both* tend to

1. be analytical

2. give unsolicited advice

3. withhold empathy

4. withhold feelings

5. be independent

6. be competitive

7. be non-verbal and

8. emotionally abandon loved ones when distressed.

Why doesn't this sound as if it will lead to a particularly good prognosis for male-male relationships? Of course these traits do not describe all men at all times. And, to some degree, gay men are often less typical. We all have gay friends who use more than 20,000 words per day! But, in general, men in Western cultures—gay or straight— tend to avoid communicating their feelings, leading to one of the major challenges *two* men face in creating intimate connections.

Gay men, in particular, grow up with a sense that they are different, and that difference is not embraced, accepted or met with empathy by them—or the society at-large. As previously discussed, the result of this experience is a need and desire to seek external validation of who and what we are. We want to know that we have value and worth. We do not want our partners to fix us. We *do* want our partners to empathize, validate and support us and our feelings. Perhaps even more than women in heterosexual relationships, gay men look to their partners for this comfort. Unfortunately, being men, we readily give advice, but seldom validation.

Questions to Ponder:

1. Do you find yourself being a "Mr. Fix-It"—always trying to make things better for your partner, or even your friends? What kind of responses have you received? Next time, try offering a simple statement of compassion, validation and/or empathy and gauging the difference in the response.

2. Do you see other men, or your partner, as competitors or even enemies? Try allowing yourself to see and treat other men as you might a dear friend or close family member. Do you notice a shift in your relationship(s) by doing so?

3. When having emotional pain, do you or your partner go off into a cave? How would it feel to share your feelings and ask for support? How would it feel to give your partner alone time until he is ready to share his pain or problem?

Challenge #4: Anal Penetration and Sexual Compatibility

Unlike heterosexual couples, where it is assumed that the man penetrates and the woman is penetrated, sexual roles are less clearly defined when two men are sexual. There may be no penetration, only oral penetration in one or two directions, only anal penetration in one or two directions or both oral and anal penetration in one or two directions. While these matters are normally worked out over time for any given couple, it is not unusual for men to avoid communicating about what they genuinely want—or do not want.

Historically, in machismo culture, men are supposed to want to penetrate and not be penetrated. This is particularly true for certain ethnic groups where being gay is distressing enough, but being a *bottom* is out of the question. Despite the fact that a man may be oriented to receive, the taboo may be just too difficult psychologically or emotionally, and he will avoid his preferred sexual desire. You may even hear a man say he is straight because he is never receptive, but he has no problem penetrating a male partner. However, the Centers for Disease Control do not categorize people according to sexual orientation when doing HIV epidemiological studies. They refer to "men who have sex with men," "men who have sex with women," "men who have sex with both men and women," etc.

Challenge yourself, some time, to go to an Internet male meeting site that asks men to disclose their sexual preferences and take a look at how most men describe themselves. Choices are generally: top, versatile top, versatile, versatile bottom, bottom. You may find yourself asking "Where'd all the bottoms go? I never knew there were so many versatile tops!" You may also see men stating, "not looking for a bottom" or "not a top." The stigma around being a bottom is still alive and well. This stigma often enters into the male-male relationship. It is not uncommon for a couple to find their sex life declining because both are natural tops or both are natural bottoms.

Regarding anal penetration, defining what it means to be a top or a bottom is delicate and controversial. I will do

> *A bottom can be defined as a man who enjoys <u>surrendering</u> to another man....*

so here at the risk of criticism, but having reviewed these definitions with several gay male sexologists it appears to be a reasonable attempt. *A bottom can be defined as a man who enjoys <u>surrendering</u> to another man* and having his anus penetrated by his partner's penis, finger, hand, fist, dildo and/or other stimulus. He enjoys the stimulation of his prostate gland and the thousands of pleasure-producing anal nerve endings, but it is the emotional and psychological *opening* to allow a partner to enter and unite with him that creates joy and defines a true bottom.

A top can be defined as a man who enjoys joining with his partner by entering, and, in doing so, <u>caring for</u> his partner and his partner's pleasure and sense of well-being. He enjoys the physical pleasure to his penis, but what defines the true top is the joy he receives by *sharing his sexual energy* with his partner and seeing his partner's responsiveness.

> *A top can be defined as a man who enjoys joining with his partner by entering, and, in doing so, <u>caring for</u> his partner....*

John and Rick, both in their forties, began dating and admitted right off that they were both tops. But, they really liked each other and said they could be versatile in order to make the relationship work. Right from the start, John was acting as the receptive partner, and he initially found it to be enjoyable. After six months, John admitted in therapy that he resented Rick never allowing him to "top" and that he honestly didn't like "to get fucked." As we explored the reasons John was allowing himself to continue to be anally receptive when it did not feel authentic to him, we stumbled on a co-dependent pattern in all of John's past relationships. John was a caregiver, and this often showed up as caring for the needs or desires of his partners to the detriment or neglect of his own needs or desires. In this relationship, by allowing himself to be penetrated, John was caring for Rick and neglecting his own sexual needs.

John and Rick's relationship exemplifies the importance of understanding that sexual role is more complex than simply positioning, physical pleasure or control. It cannot be ignored or devalued without harm to the intimacy in a gay relationship. I cringe when I hear men say, "Everyone should learn to be versatile." This is no more credible than saying, "Everyone should learn to be bisexual." There is reason to believe that one's sexual role is hardwired in one's sexual template (extensively explained in Chapter Two) and is no more a choice than sexual orientation.

It is PC (politically correct) today to be versatile, and if one is truly versatile then he will want to experience sex as *both* a top and a bottom. Limitation to one or the other for the truly versatile man may present sexual problems for a couple, as well. And, of course, some men are not anally inclined at all. Communicating with your partner about sexual roles is essential and needs to happen early and continuously in an intimate relationship. As the saying goes, "Two bottoms do not make a top!" (In Part Two of this book we will further address the "ins and outs" of anal penetration.)

HIV status also plays a critical role in a gay couple's comfort level with anal sex. It is widely accepted that anal penetration is the primary route, *but not the only route*, of transmission for HIV. The fear of infection for an HIV-negative man—or the fear of re-infection or infecting a negative partner for an HIV-positive man—is real and has a psychological, emotional and behavioral impact on gay relationships and intimacy.

All sexual behavior carries some risk. However, receptive anal intercourse puts one at the greatest risk for HIV transmission. The anal tissues are delicate, can be torn by penetration, and provide a place for the virus to hang out for a while inside the body. Minimizing this risk requires the use of sufficient lubrication and latex protection throughout intercourse.

Sometimes men who are naturally tops trying to be bottoms find penetration uncomfortable, painful, difficult or impossible. In the process they often get "ripped open" because it is so hard for them to take on the surrender role. Bottoms that are essentially raped, forced to open too quickly or use insufficient lubrication also are at serious risk for torn anal tissues. These are key factors to understand in minimizing the risk of transmission of HIV and reinforce the need to be honest with your partner about your authentic sexual role.

Questions to Ponder:

1. How important is anal penetration to you? Are you a top, bottom or truly versatile? Does your partner know? If not, why not?

2. Have you ever tried to take a sexual role that is not authentic to you? Why did you try? What happened? Would you do it differently now?

Challenge #5: HIV

The only way to have no-risk sex is to have no sex.

While HIV is not a "gay disease" it poses some serious challenges for gay men and their relationships. *The only way to have no-risk sex is to have no sex.* In any relationship, it is essential to discuss the HIV status of both partners and take necessary precautions to minimize the risk of transmission. This means, of course, that you need to know your own HIV status, which is tested for by looking for HIV antibodies. "Antibodies" are proteins that the immune system produces in response to foreign bodies (like viruses). When you have an HIV test, they are actually testing for antibodies, not the virus itself. Unfortunately, it can take from several weeks to several months after HIV exposure for these antibodies to be produced in your bloodstream in sufficient numbers to be picked up by the test. This means that there is a window of time when someone may test negative, even though there actually is virus present. As such, you cannot trust just one HIV test to give you an accurate reading of your status.

If you are entering a new sexual relationship—or you are in an open relationship—you MUST maintain safer sex practices to minimize your risk. I will leave it up to others, including your physician, to specify the details of safer sex. At a minimum, we are referring to the use of latex protection for all anal penetration which has been shown to reduce the risk of infection so long as the condoms are used consistently and correctly and remain intact throughout penetration. If you are in a totally trusting, exclusively monogamous relationship, and have had a series of HIV tests over a period of three to six months, you may consider unprotected sex after receiving the advice and counsel of your physician. (We will be discussing "totally trusting" relationships in greater detail later in this book.)

The word "monogamous" is used in this book to mean that an individual is having exclusive sex only with his partner, although the word actually means "married to one person"—as opposed to "polygamous," meaning married to several partners. This is a notable distinction as some men say they want to marry (be "monogamous"), but they do not necessarily mean sexual exclusivity.

Jimmy and Oscar, men in their forties, both physicians, met and began dating. As doctors, they both understood the implications of unsafe anal intercourse. Oscar was a true bottom and Jimmy a true top, and they knew from the first encounter that they were very compatible sexually. They initially used condoms for protection, and they discussed their HIV statuses, disclosing to one another that they were negative. Trusting each other's word, the couple moved in together and began having unprotected anal sex. After living together for nearly a year, Jimmy found a medicine vial in the bathroom with antiviral medication prescribed for Oscar. When confronted, Oscar admitted he was HIV positive and had been for ten years. Oscar admitted that he had lied, fearing that if Jimmy was aware of his positive status he would not have stayed in the relationship. Jimmy was devastated by the betrayal, but assumed he was safe from infection because he was exclusively the top in this relationship. Unfortunately, Jimmy *did* seroconvert. The relationship did not survive, and Jimmy was left to deal with the loss of the man he loved and thought he could trust, as well as the aftermath of dealing with HIV for the rest of his life.

> ~
> *Education and knowledge do not protect people from being human.*
> ~

Oscar and Jimmy's story is replete with powerful lessons. *Education and knowledge do not protect people from being human.* We all want to trust and be trusted in our relationships. Despite Ronald Reagan's failure to take any action during his presidency to address the emerging HIV/AIDS crisis, we can ironically heed the advice of his favorite Russian proverb: "Trust, but verify." Do not take chances on your health. *Get tested regularly, and discuss HIV and your sexual practices regularly with your partner.* Additionally, tops CAN—and do—get infected by having unprotected anal intercourse. It is clearly not as risky as it is for the receptive partner, but it is not risk-free.

To repeat, the only risk-free sex is *no* sex. If you want to have sex, you must realize you are taking some risks. Do everything you can to minimize your exposure. And realize that intimacy requires full honesty and discussion regarding HIV to maintain physical and emotional safety.

Questions to Ponder:

1. Does possible HIV infection or re-infection play a significant role in your decision to have anal sex? Do you fully communicate with your partner(s) about your fears and concerns? Are you taking an active role in preventing the spread of HIV and other STDIs?

2. Have you ever stayed in a relationship that was not working for you because of your fear of HIV? Do you understand how you may have been at risk even in that relationship?

3. What steps can you take to minimize your risk of HIV infection or re-infection? Are you *consistently* using safer sex precautions?

Challenge #6: Testosterone

My grandmother used to say, *"A penis has no brain."* This statement speaks volumes about the nature of male sexuality. Men are naturally and normally sexually driven. Of course there are vast differences between men, but—generally speaking—the male animal has sex on the brain frequently throughout the day, and testosterone is the hormone dominating the biological urge to "spread your seed."

In a heterosexual relationship, this drive is thwarted by the rules of the monogamous marriage paradigm—with its roots embedded in the agricultural society's economic need for family structure as well as traditional religious doctrine. In this paradigm, women marry men hoping the institution of marriage will bring with it stability, security and a nurturing home for their children. Men marry woman hoping the institution will keep other men from invading their territories—and their wives—and guarantee paternity. Women are often the energetic force for committed monogamy. Men, socialized differently, often have a tougher time than women committing to monogamy because they are given more permission by society to enjoy sexual adventure and variety. As previously discussed, men also tend to be independent and competitive. For a thorough understanding of the origins of monogamous coupling, I highly recommend *Sex at Dawn: The Prehistoric Origins of Modern Sexuality*, by Christopher Ryan and Cacilda Jetha.

In gay male relationships, the dynamic is much different. Lacking this feminine energetic force for exclusivity, hormones rage and, with no real model except traditional

"A penis has no brain."

heterosexual marriage to follow, men find themselves often conflicted and confused.

We will discuss this matter fully in Part Three of this book, but for now suffice it to say that a big challenge for the gay male couple is what do to with this normal drive to connect sexually with other men. The importance of honest communication in this arena is vital to maintaining satisfaction and assuring the well-being of an intimate gay relationship.

Questions to Ponder:

1. Have you and your partner talked about your sex life, your sex drive, and your sexual interest (or no interest) in other men? If not, what might that discussion include and how do you imagine it would feel? If yes, what feelings came up and did you feel closure upon the discussion's conclusion?

2. Do you (and/or your partner) have any relationship role models you feel comfortable emulating? Have you discussed these with your partner to see if you are on the same page? If not, why not? If so, are you satisfied with the way you both deal with your sexual feelings and the communication about sexual feelings?

Challenge #7: Alcohol, Substance Abuse and Mental Health

The use of alcohol and drugs in the gay community has become an enormous challenge for couples attempting to create intimate connections. According to PFLAG, 55% of gay men will have a substance abuse problem sometime in their lives. Gay culture was built, in part, around the bar scene, and alcohol is what bars are all about. I have had many men in my practice who drink three to four drinks each day, even more on the weekends, and don't think that is very much booze. Others, when asked if they use drugs, will say "no," but later report that they smoke marijuana when they have sex. And, methamphetamine, used to loosen inhibition and boundaries during sex, is prevalent in gay culture today due to its extremely addicting quality. Methamphetamine brain damage recovery and repair can take fourteen to twenty-four months, and—in some instances—injury is irreversible. Additionally, as the drug is often used during sex, an attempt to disconnect the sex-meth association can be formidably challenging. The result is often devastating to any attempts to create relational intimacy.

A certified addiction professional colleague of mine says people use and abuse drugs and alcohol when they are unable to express their feelings and emotions. As previously discussed, gay men mostly grow up and live in an oppressive environment. As such, they often experience internalized homophobia and heterosexism resulting in unexpressed anger, resentment and sadness in their hearts. Pushing away or denying feelings only creates more pain. *Self-medicating the pain away creates barriers to authentic human connection.* A truly intimate relationship cannot exist when either partner is under the influence of mind-altering chemicals, including alcohol. If you are using daily, looking forward all day to those cocktails at night or waiting all week for that joint, snort, smoke, bump or slam on the weekend, there is a problem that needs professional help before you can ever think about creating a deeper, more meaningful, intimate experience with a partner.

While addiction and compulsive behavior are challenges not exclusive to gay couples, it is worth noting at this point that mental illness of any type poses challenging obstacles to intimacy. It is estimated that, at any given time, 25% of the American population is suffering from some form of mental illness. If you and/or your partner is/are dealing with depression, anxiety, any obsessive-compulsive illness

Self-medicating the pain away creates barriers to authentic human connection.

(including sexual compulsion, gambling, workaholism, eating disorders, etc.), attention deficit issues or personality disorders, professional attention is essential for relationship growth and intimacy.

Questions to Ponder:

1. How much do you drink on a weekly basis? Do you use recreational drugs regularly? Do you ever drink or drug to reduce anxiety about your relationship or to avoid expressing your feelings to your partner? How would it feel to have a conversation with your partner about your drug and/or alcohol use?

2. Have you and/or your partner ever used or considered using crystal meth? Do you know anyone who has? What are the implications of its use?

3. Have you or your partner ever been in therapy? Have you discussed the possibility as a way to deal with some of the challenges in your relationship or any mental health issues you may be facing? What fears or concerns come up for you when you think about the possibility of working with a professional counselor?

Chapter Two

Where Did the Passion Go? How Sexual Intimacy Evolves or Dissolves

Manny, a very attractive and intelligent forty-five-year-old gay man, came into therapy without his partner George to deal with the problems in their eleven-year relationship.

> *Manny:* I love George. He's my best friend. I trust him more than I trust anyone in the world. When we first met we fucked like bunny rabbits. Now, we still cuddle and snuggle up on the couch together, but we never passionately kiss or have sex anymore. Occasionally we try, but it doesn't really work. Our relationship is supposed to be sexually exclusive, but I have had occasion to step out and get some sex, and I've taken advantage of it. I feel bad about that, but I want sex in my life. I don't think George cheats, you know, fools around, but who knows? Anyway, I feel I'm cheating, I mean, I know I'm cheating on George, but I feel like I'm cheating myself. Am I settling by staying with George?

Therapist: That's an intense internal struggle. There's a great deal of conflict and confusion in your heart. What do you mean by "settling?"

Manny: Well, I know I can find another man. I know this sounds terrible, but, well, I know I'm attractive enough to meet someone I find attractive and can have hot sex with. So, I guess I wonder if I'm settling for being with someone I no longer find attractive sexually.

Therapist: I see. How long has it been since you've had a good sexual connection with George?

Manny: Well, I think it was a gradual thing, but it's been at least five years since we've been really sexual.

Therapist: What was going on in your lives at that time?

Manny: Hmmm. Well, about six years ago George lost his job and had to change careers. He seemed to have lost his self-confidence, which had always been very appealing to me, and he never would open up to me about how he was feeling. Of course, at the time, his interest in sex decreased, and my interest in having sex with George declined, too. Even though George eventually got his footing and started feeling better about himself, the physical part of our relationship seemed to be damaged for good. I mean, we never fight or anything, but we're kind of distant in a way. I can't really describe it. It's like we're there for each other, and we do everything together, but there's, like, a barrier between us or something.

Manny's story illustrates the evolution or, shall we say, *devolution* of many male-male relationships. The connection starts out very passionate and sexual and, over time, the couple find themselves more friends than lovers. Understanding this process is key to avoiding the pitfalls that lead to the so-called "bed-death" phenomenon (a loss of sexual passion) in gay relationships.

So what did happen to Manny's sexual connection with George? To understand the process we need to begin at the beginning. What created the passion in the first place? There are essentially two sources of energetic attraction that ignite the spark when two people meet and feel passion—that feeling of a strong and overwhelming attraction both sexually and emotionally toward another man. The first source is your Sexual Template; the other is your Imago.

Your Sexual Template

> ~
>
> *The Sexual Template can be defined as the total of all of your sexually erotic desires.*
>
> ~

The first source of energetic attraction creating passion is the Sexual Template. The concept was originally conceived as the *Love Map* by Johns Hopkins sexologist Dr. John Money. The idea of a *template* was coined and developed by renowned sexologist Dr. William Granzig. I am expanding upon the original intent of his work to help men understand the evolution and devolution of their sexual desires. *The Sexual Template can be defined as the total of all of your sexually erotic desires.* Everyone's sexual template is different. Your unique sexual template consists of all of your erotic interests (i.e., attributes and characteristics in others and intimate activities) that stimulate sexual desire specifically in you. It has both conscious and unconscious components and, as such, we are aware of many aspects of our own template and unaware of others.

In order to understand the nature of your unique sexual template, you must first look at your sexual *cathexis*. Cathexis is fancy medical terminology simply meaning the sex you are drawn to emotionally and sexually. (We often incorrectly use the word "gender" rather than "sex" today, but gender actually means masculine or feminine, not male or female.) The definition most dictionaries give for the word "homosexual" is "of, relating to, or characterized by a tendency to direct sexual desire toward another of the same sex." This common definition is wholly inadequate and reflects the general societal misunderstanding of gay connections. Homosexuality involves affection, emotion *and* sexual attraction. Your cathexis, then, is either toward men, toward women or toward both men and women. If you only find men erotically desirable, then only men would be in your sexual template.

Next, as you move toward understanding your sexual template, you want to explore the physical attributes in others that create erotic desire for you. You may be attracted to tall men or muscular men or blond men or bearded men or black men. Note that you may find equally desirous tall men and short men, or blonds and brunets, or black men and white men. These are not conflicting attributes; they just broaden the range of interests for you erotically. You may have a very wide template—incorporating many desirous attributes—or a very narrow one with relatively few attributes. Where many individuals get confused in thinking about their template is that *finding someone attractive is* not *the same as desiring someone sexually.* For example, you may find blond hair an attractive attribute on a man, but that does not mean you necessarily find blond men sexually appealing. More pointedly, you may find a curvaceous woman attractive to look at but, as a gay man, you have no sexual desire for her.

> *...finding someone attractive is* not *the same as desiring someone sexually.*

In connection with physical attributes in the sexual template are body modifications. These may include tattoos, body piercings and jewelry serving to adorn or erotically enhance the physical body.

Next, you want to examine demeanor. You may be drawn to men who are confident or controlling or energetic or humble or mellow or passive. You may desire a man who is effeminate or one who is very masculine. Some men find power or money erotically charged. Once again, we are not talking about someone who fits the bill for an ideal *relationship*, i.e., "I want a partner with money." However, if money is a "sexual attractor" it is then considered to be in your sexual template.

Then we look at age. Some men are attracted to men of all ages. Some older men are drawn only to young men. Some young men only like older guys, and, again, not necessarily because the mature man offers wealth and stability (unless wealth and stability are in the young man's sexual template). A young man can find the physical attributes of aging men sexually erotic. (And, by the way, this is quite common in male-male connections.) Generally, however, age in the sexual template appears to "float"—staying within five years (older and younger) of one's current age.

Culture, race and religion also are factors in the sexual template. Once again, I caution you not to think in terms of the ideal mate, i.e., "I'd like to be with a partner of the same religion," but rather one's spirituality can be an erotic attractor.

One's sexual template may include socially acceptable erotic desires such as affection, tenderness, friendship, and caretaking as well as the normophilic desire for vaginal, oral and anal sex. "Normophilic" refers to sexual activity that is generally accepted by societal standards. (Anal sex still has societal taboos associated with it, but today, along with vaginal and oral sex, is considered normophilic.) Paraphilic sexual activity (i.e., exhibitionism, fetishism, bondage, masochism, sadism, transvestism, voyeurism, etc.), on the other hand, can also be in one's sexual template, even though it is often considered unacceptable or antisocial by societal standards. Sexual role preference for gay men (top, bottom, versatile) is also embedded in one's sexual template.

While we may be able to consciously figure out the contents of our sexual template, we cannot—and do not—consciously deposit or add attributes into the template. For example, you may discover that you have a recently acquired sexual desire for redheads. But you cannot wake up one morning and say to yourself, "from now on I will be erotically drawn to redheads." As gay men we are quite aware that we did not choose our cathexis. We did not choose to be gay (i.e., choose to be drawn sexually and emotionally to men), but we discovered this about ourselves along life's path.

Each person's sexual template is constantly and unconsciously expanding, but once an attribute is in the template it is there for life. We cannot "cure" our gay sexual orientation. We cannot undo an erotic shoe fetish. We can *choose*, however, which aspects of our eroticism to explore or not explore, and we make these decisions all the time both consciously and unconsciously.

The relative value of any given attribute or desire in the template does appear to change over time. For example, once, in a discussion with several gay men in their twenties, the question was posed by one of the young men, "What is the most important quality you want in a boyfriend?" One of the men said without hesitation, "Eyebrows." Evidently, this man's sexual template had well-groomed eyebrows as a top priority. It may well be assumed that at age forty some other characteristic of desire will be more important, but eyebrows will always be an erotic attractor for this man.

In general, the more your partner's erotically desirous characteristics and interests—at any given point in time—are matched and compatible with erotically desirous characteristics and interests in your sexual template, particularly highly desirous ones, the greater your sexual desire for him. I like to say when a partner matches up with your sexual template in this way, he then "fits into" your template, is "in your template" or is a "sexual template match."

28

Exercise One: Mapping Your Sexual Template

Create a list of your sexual desires, being sure to include your sexual cathexis, as well as any erotically desired physical characteristics, body modifications, demeanor, age range, ethnicity and race, religion and spirituality, normophilic desires, paraphilic desires, emotional desires, sexual roles and positions, personality, power, money and intelligence. Remember: *the sexual template contains desired characteristics that create erotic responses in you and are not characteristics that you feel would be nice to have in a mate.* Once you have your list, see if you can rate your desires on a "one-to-three" scale, of low, moderately desirable and highly desirable.

Questions to Ponder:

1. As you were mapping your sexual template did you notice how your current and past partners match your list?

2. Can you recall how your template has expanded over time? Have your desires changed? What about the relative importance of those desires?

Your Imago

The second source of energetic attraction igniting passionate connections, the Imago, is described by Harville Hendrix in his book *Getting the Love You Want*. This best-selling classic began a movement in couple's therapy considered by many to be the standard of care today. Hendrix explains that the Imago, from the word *image,* represents both the positive and negative characteristics of our primary caretakers (often our parents) growing up. We unconsciously find ourselves passionately drawn to partners who are our Imago, people who have both the positive and negative attributes of our parents. In other words, as the saying goes, "We marry our parents." This connection is referred to as our "Imago match."

We are mostly unaware (unconscious) of the fact that the people who most attract us emotionally and sexually, from the moment we meet them, are people who can drive us crazy just like our parents. *Our most passionate connections are with the men who know exactly how to push the hottest of our hot buttons and we chose them to do just that!* And, the stronger the Imago match (i.e., partners who are most like our parents and who most closely recreate the dynamics of our parent-child relationships) the stronger the passionate connection. Hendrix would say we are attracted to our Imago so we have an opportunity to heal our childhood wounds and restore a sense of wholeness that is our birthright. During the first eighteen months (approximately) of our relationships we tend to overlook a new partner's negative characteristics. Thereafter, the negative parental attributes kick in, and the proverbial shit hits the fan. What happens thereafter can mean the difference between a relationship continuing or ending *and* can mean the difference between a sexual connection continuing or ending.

What everyone wants is a high passion-low conflict relationship, but that does not exist! The greater the passion in a connection, the higher the conflict. *Relationships are either high passion-high conflict, low passion-low conflict or some gradation thereof.* Love is the glue that keeps relationships together, but relationships are not built on love. *Relationships are built on conflict resolution. The stifling of conflict, tension and pain in a relationship creates stagnation and distancing.*

Our most passionate connections are with the men who know exactly how to push the hottest of our hot buttons and we chose them to do just that!

Relationships are built on conflict resolution. The stifling of conflict, tension and pain in a relationship creates stagnation and distancing.

Exercise Two: Exploring Your Imago

Create a list of all of the positive and negative characteristics of your parents or primary caregivers based on your memories of them as a child. In other words, these descriptors do not describe them *now*, but as you experienced them when you were growing up. Once you have your list, go back and check off all of those characteristics that also describe your current partner and/or past boyfriend(s).

(The above exercise was adapted from *Getting the Love You Want Workbook* by Harville Hendrix and Helen LaKelly Hunt.)

Questions to Ponder:

1. Based on the Imago exercise, did you marry your parents? How have the negative characteristics created conflict in your relationship?

2. On a scale of one to ten, how would you rate the level of conflict and tension in your relationship? On a scale of one to ten, how would you rate the level of passion in your relationship?

3. Do you have a high passion-high conflict relationship, low passion-low conflict relationship or something moderate? What do you imagine it would be like to discuss this with your partner?

Evolution of a Relationship

Let's take a look at the flow chart in Appendix One to better understand the evolution of a relationship. The evolution takes the same path for gay and straight passionate connections. We see that the factors that bring a couple together passionately are the previously defined Imago match and Sexual Template match. *Inherent in passionate connections are conflict, tension and pain. In fact, the word* passion comes from the Latin "to suffer." It is highly unlikely for two people who are unique individuals to create a union without some energetic discord. This energy of discord creates potentiality. Ideally, the potentiality results in healing and growth for the individuals and the couple. In my opinion, *the primary purpose of a passionate, intimate relationship is to support and encourage emotional growth and development in one another.*

How a couple deals with conflict, tension and pain determines whether the relationship, the passionate sexual connection, and the intimacy will grow or stagnate. In Chapter One, we discussed how many men tend to close down when faced with difficult feelings. When one or both partners withdraw and choose not to address tough emotional issues, the energy between the men is internally dissipated. One or both stuff away the conflict, tension and/ or pain and a barrier goes up between the men. Holding back, withdrawing, denying or defending are tools used to avoid the fear of facing the feelings.

Why are we afraid? There are three fundamental reasons men fail to express their feelings. The first is fear of hurting the men we love. Often what needs to be said is not pretty. We know it may create pain in our partner to hear that something does not feel good. Second, we fear hurting the relationship. I often hear men say, "I don't want to rock the boat. Things seem to be going along just fine (low conflict), and if I bring up some contentious issue the relationship may not survive." The third fear is of being rejected or abandoned—we do not want to be left to deal with our issues, or our lives, all alone.

The questions you need to ask yourself when fears arise are:

1. Wouldn't I be hurting my partner more by distancing myself emotionally than I would be by sharing my pain?

> *...the primary purpose of a passionate, intimate relationship is to support and encourage emotional growth and development in one another.*

2. Do I trust the man I love and this relationship enough to know that our partnership can survive a discussion of my pain?

3. What feels more alone than holding pain inside, unable to share it with the man I love?

> ~
> **When you act out of fear, you block the energy of love.**
> ~

The opposite of love is not hate, it is fear. Fear keeps you from loving. Love and fear cannot occupy the same space in your heart at the same time. *When you act out of fear, you block the energy of love.* You close down the possibility for true intimacy.

> ~
> **Intimacy is directly proportional to vulnerability.**
> ~

Intimacy is the closeness that results when people make themselves vulnerable with one another. *Intimacy is directly proportional to vulnerability.* Think about how much closer you feel to a friend or loved one after you share a private thought or feeling. In a relationship, when you hold back feelings out of fear (or for any reason) you resist vulnerability and shut off the intimate connection. Over time the result of this shutting down is sexual disconnection. Relationships of this type frequently go into contentment-resentment mode, where there is surface contentment with internal resentment. The couple begins to "play house" and focuses on making the external environment and appearance look perfect, while the internal dynamic suffocates and dies. Hendrix would describe this shut-down as an avoidance of healing dialogue and "a festering of childhood wounds." Ambivalence and doubt about the relationship creep in. The partnership stagnates—with no growth for the individuals or the couple often leading to co-dependency, addictions or dissolution of the relationship.

The decision to choose love over fear means addressing conflict, tension and pain. When you take the path on the left side of the flow chart you find there is honesty with yourself and your partner. Openness, availability, empathy, compassion, appreciation and validation characterize the manner of communication and dialogue. Allowing yourself to share pain, address conflict and confront tension opens your heart and creates vulnerability. It is emotionally risky, but the reward is a heightened level of intimacy with your partner.

After pushing through fear by taking the route of love, opening your heart and sharing your feelings with an available partner, resolution brings with it healing, trust, renewed commitment, a sense of safety, and the passion necessary for enhanced sexual connection. The individuals—and the couple—experience growth, and the couple feels very much in love.

The great irony facing passionate partners is that the more you try to keep the relationship and your partner safe, the less safe the relationship becomes. The greatest risk to intimacy is trying to protect yourself, your partner or the relationship by avoiding conflict and confrontation. Even more ironic is that men who fear addressing sexual problems and avoid the issue feel they do so in order to protect the safety of the relationship. This protection actually helps to further erode the sexual connection. Safety is required for intimacy, but *safety grows out of surviving emotional vulnerability with your partner.*

In Chapter Three we will focus on how to communicate with your partner to resolve conflict, tension and pain. But, for now, let's imagine you have been engaged in effective dialogue with your partner and have resolved a particular issue. Trust, commitment, safety and passion are renewed. Recall that, inherent in a passionate relationship, are conflict, tension and pain. So, it won't be long before there will be the need to address a new challenge with your partner. This relationship loop is necessary to maintain the movement of energy for both passion and intimacy.

Oftentimes men have a more difficult time with the concept of loops and cycles than women do. Women tend to do much better with Imago work than men because it is emotion-driven and cyclic in nature. Women's lives are more about

The great irony facing passionate partners is that the more you try to keep the relationship and your partner safe, the less safe the relationship becomes.

...safety grows out of surviving emotional vulnerability with your partner.

cycles than are the lives of men. Men tend to think linearly, women tend to think cyclically. Women have monthly menstrual cycles and their orgasms can often be multiple. As such, most women are driven sexually by an emotional energy that builds upon itself to heightened cyclic orgasmic response. Men are driven physically toward reaching singular climax and then collapse. The chart depicting the Evolution of a Relationship asks men to think more cyclically and emotionally than linearly and physically.

Questions to Ponder:

1. Do you and your partner address the conflict, tension and pain in your relationship? On which side of the Evolution of a Relationship flow chart do you guys find yourselves?

2. If you find yourself avoiding, holding back or withdrawing, what fear or fears come up for you that prevent you from engaging with your partner? How is disengaging more detrimental to your intimate connection?

3. How did you feel the last time you revealed some very private thought or feeling to your partner or a close friend?

Discussing Desire

Returning now to the sexual template aspect of our model, you may be asking how desire plays a role in the continuum of sexual connection. Let's first look at what is known to sexologists as the "sexual response" cycle. (There's that pesky word "cycle" again! More on that in a moment.) Essentially there are four phases to sex. The first phase is *desire*. Without sexual desire, nothing happens. As previously explained, when there is desire, some attribute—or attributes—in one's sexual template correspond(s) to some attribute—or attributes—that the potential sex partner has to offer. The triggered erotic desire is the result of the sexual template match. (Note that for many men simply the thought of having sex with a new, risky or anonymous partner can trigger desire. If there is a very minimal template match, subsequent sexual meetings and/or sexual sustainability become unlikely.) Once in phase one, if engagement occurs, then phase two, *arousal*, kicks in. Arousal is the "play time" of sex. This is the longest physical phase and is characterized by kissing, holding, petting, sucking, intercourse, etc. At some point during arousal, men typically get close to climax. There is a point of no return after which the third phase, *orgasm*, takes place. This phase lasts six to eight seconds and then it is over. Phase four is *resolution*, which, for men, is a refractory stage, meaning there needs to be a period of time to regroup before one can climax again.

So, then, without desire, without a sexual template match, the sexual response cycle does not even get started. If you meet a man with long hair and thin stature—which are strongly desired sexually by you—and three years later he cuts his hair and gains fifty pounds, what do you imagine would happen to your desire? Or, if twenty years ago you entered into a relationship with a slender man who had a large, uncircumcised penis—both of which you strongly desired at the time—but now you're much more desirous of muscled guys with big biceps, what do you imagine would happen to your desire for your lanky but well-endowed mate? Whether your partner "falls out" of your sexual template (i.e., he no longer fits into your template), or your template expands leaving your partner behind, the challenges posed by our changing partners and our growing desires are among the most difficult tension spots for couples to discuss. But…just as we discussed with all conflict, tension and pain in relationships, empathic, open and honest dialogue is necessary if there is any hope of maintaining intimacy and sexual connection.

At the first sign of decreased desire you need to ask yourself: Is there some emotionally charged issue I'm not addressing? Has there been a change in one or more of my partner's desirous attributes? Has my sexual template expanded to a degree that it has left my partner behind? Am I avoiding discussion about a template problem with my partner?

Aside from expanding emotional intimacy by opening up difficult dialogue, there frequently are things that can be done to rectify a changing template problem. Losing weight, re-growing a beard or shaving hair are relatively easy template remedies and—sometimes—the answer may be as easy as that.

I'll often hear men say, "But that's so superficial." And I respond, "No, that's *human*." And it's honest. Deceiving yourself into believing that your sexual interest in certain physical attributes doesn't matter simply shuts down the sexual response cycle with your partner. For circumstances that cannot be changed, it is still vitally important to communicate with your partner about these issues. For example, if you are a template-driven top and your partner can no longer bottom due to some medical problem, it is important to talk about the feelings that arise and how you are going to proceed sexually as a couple. Ignoring or devaluing the problem creates the 900-pound gorilla in the room that comes between you and your partner. True intimacy suffers as emotional distance grows. The manner in which we communicate and dialogue around tough issues will be addressed in Chapter Three, and Part Two of this book will help you work on the sexual connection with your partner.

Questions to Ponder:

1. Has your template outgrown your partner, or has your partner fallen out of your template? What changes have occurred?

2. Is the desire phase of the sexual response cycle a problem for you in your relationship? If so, what factors do you see as obstacles to desire both in terms of confronting conflict, tension and pain *and* your sexual template match?

3. What do you imagine it would be like to have a dialogue with your partner about the challenges you face in your sexual relationship? What fears would you have to face to have that discussion?

Sustainable Sexual Intimacy

In summary, there are five points to assimilate in order to understand the nature of a sustainable sexually intimate connection:

1. An Imago match (a connection with a man who unconsciously stirs up childhood wounds) and a Sexual Template match (a connection with a man who possesses multiple characteristics that create erotic desire) are generally necessary preconditions for a sustainable intimate and passionate connection.

2. The sexual template is constantly and unconsciously expanding; while individual characteristics cannot be removed from the template, the relative importance of any particular erotic desire can change with time. As such, it is possible for a partner to fall out of your sexual template or for you to lose sexual interest if sexual desires not attributable to your partner become more potent.

3. Erotic desires embedded in the template are not consciously chosen. If chosen, many men in loving relationships with waning sexual interest would make the choice to be erotically connected to their current partner rather than look for sex elsewhere.

WHERE DID THE PASSION GO?

A fundamental point regarding the sexual template concept is that *if your loving partner has lost sexual interest in you it is <u>not</u> because he has made a <u>conscious</u> decision to no longer find you sexually desirous.*

> ~
>
> *...if your loving partner has lost sexual interest in you it is <u>not</u> because he has made a <u>conscious</u> decision to no longer find you sexually desirous.*
>
> ~

4. Men are often aroused by the very idea of sex or the environment in which they have an opportunity for a sexual encounter. As such, it is possible to have a highly enjoyable sexual experience with a man with whom there is a fleeting contextual attraction but a weak sexual template match. Such contextual encounters are generally not sustainable.

5. *Sexual sustainability generally requires a Sexual Template match and an Imago match in which the emotional connection is growing and developing as a result of vulnerably engaging dialogue around relational conflict, tension and pain.*

If you find yourself in a relationship without a strong sexual template match that might have been built on a sexual contextual connection or solely on an emotional connection, this does *not* mean the relationship is of less value, is less legitimate or not sustainable. Rather, it is important to acknowledge what is honestly happening sexually and to engage in open dialogue about what each partner wants to do about any sexual desire issue that arises in the relationship.

So, let's go back to Manny's story. See if you can now understand the reasons for Manny's sexual connection problems with George.

There are two major components causing the breakdown. The first is a sexual template issue. Manny was very attracted to George's sense of self-confidence, which changed when he lost his job. This change in demeanor resulted in a subsequent loss of desire adversely affecting their connection.

The second component is related to the fact that George closed down emotionally after he lost his job. He had great difficulty discussing his feelings with Manny. A wall went up, shutting down the energetic connection and leading to a low conflict-low passion relationship.

Manny and George must now pick up the pieces by talking about the feelings as they have unfolded over the past five to six years. You can imagine what a formidable challenge this will be and how, the sooner problems are addressed, the more likely they are to be resolved.

Chapter Three

Creative Intimacy through Dialogue: Exercises for Expansive Communication of Feelings and Emotions

Judd and Eric have been dating for almost a year, and they usually spend weekend days off together. One sunny weekend afternoon, after a nice brunch at their favorite restaurant, Judd tells Eric he'd like to see the new comedy playing at the local movie theater. Judd knows Eric doesn't like comedies very much, and he figures he may have to go by himself. The following conversation ensues:

Eric: That was a terrific brunch and what a terrific day.

Judd: Totally awesome. I'm in such an up mood I'd really like to go see the comedy playing at the cineplex.

Eric: Ugh…I'd really rather be outside in the sun.

Judd: Okay, cool, well why don't you enjoy the day while I check out the movie? I know you're not much into comedies anyway.

Eric: Great. Dinner tonight at my place?

Judd: Sure, looking forward to it

Edward and Harry have been dating for almost a year and they usually spend weekend days off together. One sunny weekend afternoon, after a nice brunch at their favorite restaurant, Edward tells Harry he'd like to see the new comedy playing at the local movie theater. Edward knows Harry doesn't like comedies very much, and he figures he may have to go by himself. The following conversation ensues:

Harry: That was a terrific brunch and what a terrific day.

Edward: Totally awesome. I'm in such an up mood I'd really like to go see the comedy playing at the cineplex.

Harry: Ugh…wouldn't you rather spend this beautiful day out in the sun?

Edward: Well, I'd really like to see the movie. Why don't you enjoy the day in the sun and I'll check out the movie? I know you're not much into comedies anyway. We'll meet up later.

Harry (not happy): Well, okay, I guess.

Edward: We're still having dinner tonight together, right?

Harry: I'm…I'm not sure. Why don't you call me when you get out of the movie?

Edward: Okay. Hope to see you later, then.

How is it possible that two identical scenarios could play out so differently? Many people will look at these, side-by-side, and conclude that the first pair are more mature, trusting and understanding of each other's needs. A closer examination will uncover very common human dynamics resulting in a misunderstanding that could have been averted with better—and more empathic—communication skills. Clearly something was triggered in Harry that was not triggered in Eric.

Imagine that Harry grew up in a home where

1. you rarely were permitted to express your needs and desires

2. you hardly ever seemed to get your way

3. your parents were inconsistently available for you emotionally

4. your parents went off and did what they wanted to do when you wanted to be with them

5. on nice days you were required to stay home and do your homework rather than go out and play.

Now imagine that in Harry's last relationship

1. when things seemed to be getting serious, Harry's boyfriend started to withdraw

2. when Harry wanted to do something, his boyfriend wanted to do something different

3. when Harry's boyfriend said he was going to the gym, Harry discovered he was fooling around with another guy.

You can begin to see how Harry's previous life experiences influenced his emotional reaction to Edward's suggestion that they spend the day separately.

If you grew up in a home where your caretakers were emotionally inconsistent in their availability—sometimes hyperattentive and sometimes abandoning—you are going to have an altogether different reaction to your new boyfriend's desire for alone time (at the movies or anywhere else) than if you grew up in a home where your emotional needs were more consistently addressed and supported. If you had a previous boyfriend who lied about his whereabouts and deceived you, you are going to have a different reaction to your new boyfriend's desire for alone time than if your last boyfriend was loyal and honest.

The word "emotion" comes from an old French word for "to stir up." When emotion arises, it seems to come instantly from nowhere, and it stirs us up, both physiologically and behaviorally. We cannot control this onslaught of strong feelings. Many will tell you the key to good relationships is to "control your emotions." This is not possible. You can control how you *react to* your emotions, but the actual feelings that come up are immediate and irreclaimable.

Emotions are evoked in us as a result of some historical experiences and/or indoctrinations creating an underlying belief system that is being challenged. We have stored away, in our conscious and unconscious minds, millions of messages that are based upon what we have learned through experience or what others have told us. These messages are actually beliefs. Beliefs are simply thoughts we think over and over. *Beliefs are not absolute truths. Beliefs are personal perspectives, and we choose for ourselves which beliefs we want to hold on to and which we want to let go of.* Some beliefs serve us very well to keep us safe in our environment. Other beliefs work against us and prevent us from being all we can be and having the relationships we want in our lives.

> *Beliefs are not absolute truths. Beliefs are personal perspectives, and we choose for ourselves which beliefs we want to hold on to and which we want to let go of.*

44

Because each of us has had a different set of experiences and teachers in our lives, all of us have unique belief systems. As such, we all react to any given life situation in different ways. Harry may believe that when a boyfriend tells him that he's going to the movies on a bright sunshiny day that really means he is going to rendezvous with another man. This brings up an immediate feeling of anxiety about possible emotional abandonment and betrayal. Eric, on the other hand, might like to be outside with Judd, but he is more ready to trust because his history does not support a belief of mistrust. The feeling that comes up might be disappointment, but Eric is able to regroup quickly, knowing he will see Judd for dinner.

Many books have been written about how you can change your beliefs to improve your sense of self and your happiness. I will not go into great detail here, except to say that we are always changing our belief systems to improve our lives. For example, most gay men had a belief at one time that being gay was "bad" in some way. *In order to accept oneself as gay, one must abandon the negative beliefs about being gay.* For example, a case can be made that if you want to be happy in a relationship with someone who likes a great deal of alone time, you must abandon any beliefs that characterize your partner's independent behavior as bad, uncommitted or unsafe.

> *In order to accept oneself as gay, one must abandon the negative beliefs about being gay.*

Our work in this book, however, is more about: (1) recognizing our hot buttons, (2) identifying our triggered feelings, (3) understanding how our underlying beliefs are triggering these emotions, and (4) learning to *share* these understandings with our partners to create more connectivity, empathy, compassion and intimacy.

Exercise One: Determining Your Hot Buttons

This exercise is best to do by yourself, at least for now. We will return later to share this with your partner. Find a quiet, comfortable place to sit and reflect with no disturbances. Give yourself about thirty minutes.

Part 1 - Childhood Memories

Close your eyes and recall an emotionally distressing childhood memory. (If you find this too difficult, stop and regroup for another time or work this through with a professional.)

Allow your mind to recall the feelings. What were those feelings? (See the Inventory of Feelings in Appendix Two if you need help putting these into words.) What did you need or want at that moment that was missing? What could your caregivers/parents have provided that they did not provide at that time?

Repeat this exercise with another three or four memories.

Finally, open your eyes and complete the chart on page 47:

Determining Your Hot Buttons
Part 1 - Childhood Memories

CHILDHOOD MEMORY	FEELINGS	MISSING NEED	DESIRED FROM PARENTS
EX: Parents left me home alone often	Felt left out, unloved	Being included	Have parents take me with them
1.			
2.			
3.			
4.			
5.			

Give yourself a bit of a break and again find a safe place without distraction for another thirty minutes.

Part 2 - Relationship Memories

Close your eyes, and this time allow your mind to recall an emotionally distressing memory from a past intimate relationship.

Recall the feelings. What were they? What did you need or want at that time that was missing? What could your partner have provided that he did not provide at that time?

Repeat this exercise with another three or four memories, perhaps from the same relationship or a different one.

Open your eyes and complete the chart on page 49:

Determining Your Hot Buttons
Part 2 - Relationship Memories

RELATIONSHIP MEMORY	FEELINGS	MISSING NEED	DESIRED FROM PARTNER
EX: Boyfriend told me he was going to gym but was having an affair	Betrayal	Honesty Commitment	Sexual exclusivity
1.			
2.			
3.			
4.			
5.			

Do you notice any similarities in the two charts you filled out? Generally speaking, *the most emotionally charged situations in our adult relationships are caused by the wounds of childhood*, as explained by Harville Hendrix. He would tell us that *what we wanted and needed most in childhood is what we want and need most* in our adult relationships. However, there may be "missing needs" in your past adult relationships that are new and unlike your childhood experiences. *The important point to understand is that your hot buttons are pushed when a basic need or desire that was missing in your past is re-experienced in a current situation with your partner.*

(The above exercise was adapted from *Getting The Love You Want Workbook* by Harville Hendrix and Helen LaKelly Hunt.)

Let's begin to understand Harry as someone who (1) wanted and needed his parents to be more consistently available emotionally and spend more time with him doing the things he wanted to do as a child, and (2) wanted and needed more trust and reassurance from his partner because of a history of abandonment and betrayal. Now we can understand how Edward really pushed his hot buttons by suggesting an afternoon at the movies by himself while Harry was left to be alone on a lovely sunny weekend afternoon. The underlying belief triggered in Harry was "when my boyfriend wants time by himself he is abandoning me for someone else." The feelings that came up for Harry were real, instantaneous and charged. He tacitly expressed some disappointment, but he was terribly hurt and upset, and immediately considered punishing Edward by returning the abandonment and not seeing him for dinner. The communication is shutting down because neither Harry nor Edward comprehends why the hurt is so strong and why the hot button is so hot.

The important point to understand is that your hot buttons are pushed when a basic need or desire that was missing in your past is re-experienced in a current situation with your partner.

Both partners need to realize the historical precedents for the emotion and the resultant underlying beliefs for complete empathic communication and conflict resolution. *The main reason couples fail to engage conflict is for fear of hurting the relationship.* If Harry were to simply tell Edward he didn't want to go to the movies and that he should spend his Sunday afternoons with him—without explaining the underlying emotional discharge and beliefs—Edward's response would likely be negative.

Let's take a look at how Harry might have engaged his feelings with Edward, first without any understanding of his hot buttons and then with knowledge of his hot buttons.

> *The main reason couples fail to engage conflict is for fear of hurting the relationship.*

Version One

Harry: That was a terrific brunch and what a terrific day.

Edward: Totally awesome. I'm in such an up mood I'd really like to go see the comedy playing at the cineplex.

Harry: Ugh...wouldn't you rather spend this beautiful day out in the sun?

Edward: Well, I'd really like to see the movie. Why don't you enjoy the day in the sun and I'll check out the movie? I know you're not much into comedies anyway. We'll meet up later.

Harry: It's such a great day, why don't you want to spend the afternoon with me? You always have to have your time alone.

Edward: That's not true. We just spent the night together and had this great brunch. I just want to see this flick, I know you're not into it, so you go do your thing and I'll do mine. We'll meet up later.

Harry: I'm…I'm not sure I want to meet up later.

Edward: Oh, come on, Harry. I just want a little time for myself for a couple of hours, and I'd like to catch the movie. We spent all day together, yesterday, and I was hoping we'd spend tonight together.

Harry: Do what you want. I'll talk to you later.

Edward: Don't be that way.

Harry: What way? I told you to do what you want, didn't I?

Edward: Okay, okay. I'll call you later.

Version Two

Harry: That was a terrific brunch and what a terrific day.

Edward: Totally awesome. I'm in such an up mood I'd really like to go see the comedy playing at the cineplex.

Harry: Ugh…wouldn't you rather spend this beautiful day out in the sun?

Edward: Well, I'd really like to see the movie. Why don't you enjoy the day in the sun and I'll check out the movie? I know you're not much into comedies anyway. We'll meet up later.

Harry: You know, Edward, I feel disappointed. It's such a great day out, and I so much wanted for us to be together.

Edward: You seem really upset. Are you okay?

Harry: I guess it's one of those hot button things we've talked about in the past. You know how when I was a kid my folks would often leave me and do their own thing—and also the way Charlie used to say he was going to the gym and he really wasn't.

Edward: Hey, babe, I understand, and I feel bad about setting off such pain and doubt. You know I love you. I just thought it would be good to have a little alone time. Not because I don't want to be with you, but because I feel time apart is good for both of us and helps us appreciate each other more when we're together. And I do want to see that movie. I'm not seeing anyone else. Listen, I'll make it up to you tonight after dinner. Okay?

Harry: I love you, too. Okay. I'll see you tonight. Enjoy the movie. I think I'll take a walk in the park.

So what about *Edward's* hot buttons? How did they play out in the two scenarios?

Well, it turns out that Edward grew up with parents who were always on him about one thing or another. They were always around, his dad had his office at home and his mom was a stay-at-home mom. The family always vacationed together, and Edward was always told what to do and how to do it. Despite the family's physical proximity, there was often emotional distancing and rejecting of Edward's ideas and input, leaving him to amuse himself. What Edward wanted most growing up was to feel supported both when with his family *and* when doing his own thing independently. His underlying belief is that when another man wants a lot of time and attention, privacy and individuality are compromised and independent pursuit is unsupported. In his last dating relationship, which was intense but only lasted a few months, he felt smothered by a man who always needed to be by Edward's side and would even show up at his apartment without calling first.

Edward's hot buttons are pushed when a boyfriend is smothering or appears needy.

The fascinating and ironically cruel dynamic that often presents itself in passionate connections is opposing hot buttons. Recalling that the greater the passion in a relationship the greater the conflict, it would make sense that we are drawn to men who have the opposite challenges to our own. For this couple, when Edward wants space, Harry's hot button is pushed—and when Harry wants a lot of Edward's time, Edward's hot button is pushed.

Passionate partners are unconsciously calling out, "I'll push your hot button if you push mine!" Without the tools to understand and engage the underlying reasons for the conflict, the couple will go 'round and 'round defending their own points of view for any given problem. I often hear couples say "we've been down this road before" or "we always end up in a stand-off."

Notice, in Version Two of the Harry and Edward story, Harry begins by discussing his feelings: "You know, Edward, I feel disappointed." This is the classic "I" message or "I" statement. It is formed by using the words "I feel" followed by a feeling word (see the Inventory of Feelings in Appendix Two). Additionally, the words "you" and "your" are consciously left out of the message. *When we use a "you" statement we invite defensiveness.* For example, Harry says, "You always have to have your time alone." Of course, Edward is going to defend himself and argue his own point of view. From that point, any conversation will either escalate or shut down, but no real honest discussion of feelings will occur. For Edward and Harry, the discussion shut down and both left the brunch feeling disconnected.

Using the "I" message means making yourself vulnerable by expressing your feelings without blaming your partner for making you feel the way you do. Your partner cannot make

> *Passionate partners are unconsciously calling out, "I'll push your hot button if you push mine!"*

you feel anything, but he can—and he will—trigger hot buttons that can start a cascade of feelings. Notice how, in Version Two, Harry expresses his feelings and then lets Edward know what hot buttons were pushed. Harry takes complete responsibility for his feelings. The resultant response is non-defensive.

In fact, Edward's response has all of *the elements of a loving dialogue: empathy, validation, compassion, re-assurance, appreciation, compromise, love and honesty.* Let's take a look at each of these elements and see how Edward used them:

Empathy

Probably *the single most important part of any conversation with your partner is empathy.* Empathy is allowing yourself to feel your partner's feelings. To do so you must open both your heart and your mind. You must take the focus off of your own "stuff." When we are defending our own points of view we are paying no attention to our partners' hurt, pain, anger, frustration or discomfort. When an "I" message is used it is an opening to connect with your partner's feelings. Edward says, "I feel bad about setting off such pain and doubt" and, in doing so, creates an empathic connection.

Validation

As mentioned in Chapter One, in general, *gay men need a great deal of validation.* When we do not affirm our partners' feelings and points of view we, in essence, devalue our partners. Help your partner by acknowledging the validity of his emotional response and the way of seeing the situation from his vantage point, i.e., his history and experience. Edward tells Harry, "I understand"— he does not say that he agrees with Harry's point of view, but he validates his experience and feelings by offering understanding.

Compassion

Compassion is a sympathetic connection to your partner's hurt and a desire to help him relieve it. When you concentrate on your own hurt and want it relieved it is difficult to focus on your partner's hurt and how you are going to help him through it. *Showing compassion is a selfless expression of your love without judgment.* Edward expresses his love, calls Harry "babe," and expresses a desire to help him feel better by offering up appreciation and compromise.

Reassurance

When your partner uses an "I" message and creates vulnerability, you want to provide reassurance that doing so did not harm the relationship. You also want to listen for your partner's insecurity, and reassure him that he is safe with you. When I hear a man say his partner is "needy," the first question I ask is "Are you providing reassurance?" Edward reassures Harry by affirming his love and stating clearly, "I'm not seeing anyone else." He also tells Harry that he wants his alone time, "Not because I don't want to be with you…" Harry is then able to relax and give Edward his space. *The tension between intimacy and autonomy is a common challenge in male-male relationships. As such, the tendency to find the more intimacy-driven partner with a fear of being abandoned or rejected and the more autonomy-driven partner with a fear of being engulfed or controlled, is also commonly seen in male-male relationships.* Satisfying Edward's need for autonomy and quelling his fear of engulfment requires *reassuring* Harry that any fear of abandonment is unwarranted and that his need for intimacy is intact.

Appreciation

Letting your partner know you are grateful for him and your relationship is an essential part of reaffirming the emotional bond you share. When explaining his point of

Showing compassion is a selfless expression of your love without judgment.

The tension between intimacy and autonomy is a common challenge in male-male relationships.

view to Harry, saying "…I feel time apart is good for both of us and helps us appreciate each other more…," the word "more" suggests and expresses an appreciation that already exists for Edward.

Compromise

In order to establish some closure, both partners must give a little to reach an agreement. Mutual concession creates a confluence of the opposing interests to produce a sense of fairness and understanding. *Relationships are not about equality; they are about mutuality. Compromise is not the same as settling. Settling or giving in suggests a lack of mutuality.* When Edward says, "I'll make it up to you tonight…," he is saying he will give Harry something he wants in return. Of course, in this instance, the sexual innuendo is of mutual benefit. However, the lightness of the offer keeps Harry from feeling he is left with nothing, and offers him the opportunity to focus on something other than his fear of infidelity. The focus on making love later with Edward gives Harry the closure he needs to enjoy his afternoon.

Love

The expression of love can certainly be a verbal, "I love you," but body language, tone of voice and facial expression are even more important. Take your partner's hand, show endearment in your eyes, and be soft, slow and gentle in tone. *Give your partner your love without looking for anything in return.* We can sense from reading Edward's words that there is a sincerity of feeling backed up by the verbal expression of love, which affirms his connection with Harry.

Honesty

Total honesty is the top priority for building trust and safety. If what you have to say is not true or not *completely* true, do not say it. Be aware—being *totally* honest is not the same as being *brutally* honest. If you need to say something difficult

> *Relationships are not about equality; they are about mutuality. Compromise is not the same as settling. Settling or giving in suggests a lack of mutuality.*

> *Total honesty is the top priority for building trust and safety.*

it is time for you to use an "I" statement. Edward not only reassures Harry, but shares his own feelings about the situation. By expressing his own take on the issue, Edward is providing thoughtful, honest dialogue.

Being honest with your partner necessarily requires being honest with yourself. It is not always easy to know how to be—or even if we are being—true to ourselves. When we are ambivalent or "of two minds" it is difficult to assess what we honestly feel. Our heart may be telling us one thing and our head quite another. *Being okay with ambivalence is important for individual happiness <u>and</u> relationship happiness.* Allow yourself to open up to all sides of any tough problem and pay attention to the feelings associated with all sides. Listen to your body. Where do you feel the emotions in your body and what are the physical feelings? Feeling good expresses itself viscerally quite differently than feeling bad. Pay attention to these cues, because they will give you input about your honest feelings on all sides of any issue.

I'm not particularly fond of using scripts and techniques to communicate. They often feel unnatural and are, likely, unsustainable. You and your partner will have to come up with communication styles that work for you. At the same time, creating a conscious awareness to include these elements in your dialogue will improve connectivity and increase intimacy. More information on the use of these elements may be found in Tammy Nelson's *Getting the Sex You Want.*

There are times when a "mirroring" technique can be helpful. Often, when I see clients in therapy, I get the feeling the partners are not hearing each other accurately. You may feel this yourself when in dialogue with your partner. This is the time for mirroring. One at a time, I will ask the listening partner to "mirror back" *exactly* what the speaking partner just said—without commenting on the content or his feelings about the content. I will

Being honest with your partner necessarily requires being honest with yourself.

then ask the speaking partner "Is that exactly what you said? Was anything inaccurate? Was anything left out?" It is not unusual to find that nothing was actually heard, because the listening partner was stewing in his own rage or the content was entirely misunderstood. We repeat the exercise until the listening partner has accurately reflected back his partner's words.

At times, the mirror is accurate but the tone of the reflection sends a message that was unintended in the content. For example:

> *Bobby (sincerely spoken and directed to the therapist):* I feel hurt when I come home from work looking forward to seeing Charlie, and he is out at the bar drinking with his friend Tom.
>
> *Therapist:* Charlie, could you mirror that back to Bobby?
>
> *Charlie:* He doesn't like me drinking.
>
> *Therapist:* Bobby, is that what you said?
>
> *Bobby:* No.
>
> *Therapist:* Please turn to Charlie again and repeat what you said.
>
> *Bobby:* I feel hurt when I come home from work looking forward to seeing Charlie, and he is out at the bar drinking with his friend Tom.
>
> *Therapist:* Please direct your statement directly to Charlie.
>
> *Bobby:* I feel hurt, Charlie, when I come home looking forward to seeing you and you're out at the bar drinking with Tom.

Therapist: Good. Now, Charlie, please look at Bobby and mirror that back.

Charlie (sarcastically): You feel hurt (rolls eyes) when I'm out drinking and you come home to an empty house.

Therapist: Bobby, is that what you said?

Bobby: Not exactly.

Therapist: What exactly did you say?

Bobby: I said that if he's out...

Therapist: Please direct this to Charlie.

Bobby: Charlie, I really feel hurt when I come home wanting to see you and you're out with Tom at the bar.

Therapist: Charlie, please mirror that back, and direct it to Bobby.

Charlie (disgusted): You said you get hurt when I'm out at the bar when you get home.

Therapist: Bobby?

Bobby: That's sort of what I said.

Therapist: Was anything inaccurate or left out?

Bobby: No, but his tone of voice leads me to believe he doesn't "get" how I feel.

At this point, the therapist would do well to help the couple go back to their hot buttons to see how past experiences and childhood wounds play into the current scenario. Perhaps Charlie feels smothered in this relationship because he came from a family where he was not given freedom and independence. Bobby may feel left out and excluded when

Charlie goes off with a friend because, as a child, he was left out of certain school activities because he was perceived by the other children as different. Once the partners understand each other's hot buttons, they are often better able to hear what each has to say. The mirroring technique sometimes helps partners to see that one or the other is not being heard accurately or a critical point is being missed.

Often our partners understand what we are saying or what we need or want, but they do not understand how important those things are to us. *When something is especially important, you can address the feeling with an "it's important to me" statement.* Simply stating, "It is really important to me that we visit my parents this weekend... together," sends the message that you are more than asking for what you want. You are stating that a particular desire is important to you and to your connection with your partner. You may not get what you want, but you also verbalized your feelings and did not attempt to manipulate a situation to get a result. Remember, everything cannot be "really important" or the impact of the "it's important to me" statement is diminished.

It's not always easy to ask for what you want. Using the "I" statement as a precursor to express feelings about the conversation you are about to have can help to break the ice and relieve some of the anxiety. For example, "I'm feeling really anxious about asking you for this, but, it's really important to me that we visit my parents this weekend...together." Some feel using "I" statements is just a sophisticated form of manipulation to get what you want. It is important to be honest with yourself regarding your motives. If you are being honest about your feelings and your motivation, the use of the "I" statement is a valuable tool for taking responsibility for your feelings and expressing your needs and desires.

Setting up the environment for a serious conversation is also an important—and highly personal—component

> *When something is especially important, you can address the feeling with an "it's important to me" statement.*

of good dialogue. Of course, a significant or meaningful conversation can happen spontaneously at any time, and when a conflict arises that is hot, a couple may choose to engage at that very moment. However, if an escalation of emotion and disrespectful language ensues—or if one of the partners shuts down—it is time to *make a date to dialogue*. One of the partners would initiate a "time out" by saying that the discussion is not going in a positive direction. At that time, the two would agree to a date and time within the next few days to have a serious conversation. You do not want to put off your talk for more than three or four days. A good cool-down period is from twenty-four to forty-eight hours, and if the conflict is pushed out beyond three days people tend to dismiss or devalue it—until the next time it comes up or is thrown up in someone's face in response to another confrontation.

The "date to dialogue" is the opportunity for you to discuss how and why your hot buttons were pushed. It is a time to discuss feelings and for both parties to take responsibility for those feelings. It is a time of considerable vulnerability, and, as such, it is essential that it take place in a supportive environment created by both parties, as a couple.

Let's say Bobby and Charlie decided to talk on Friday night at 7:00. At the agreed-upon time, the partners will want to start by asking each other how they are feeling and if they are okay with proceeding with the date to dialogue. Unless there is a real problem with moving forward, which they would also want to discuss, it is time to retreat together to a place that feels safe for both partners.

So how do you begin a date to dialogue? You may have a place in your home, or—if you do not live together—a neutral place, where it is particularly conducive to talk. Some of the key elements when finding such a place are:

1. Enough light to see into each other's eyes and get a sense of facial expressions, but not so much light as

Sobriety is the only way to connect honestly with one another. If you need alcohol as a lubricant to express your feelings to the person you love, you know there is a serious problem— either in the relationship or with alcohol or both.

to be glaring. Fluorescent lighting and direct sun are probably not good ideas. Candlelight is pleasant, but probably not sufficient by itself to see each other clearly.

2. No distractions—none. No TVs, no computers, no (cell) phones. If you wish to have soft background music, it may be best not to have vocals and to play it *very* softly.

3. Don't eat or drink alcohol during the dialogue. Other beverages are fine, but you will want to have all of your faculties. *Sobriety is the only way to connect honestly with one another. If you need alcohol as a lubricant to express your feelings to the person you love, you know there is a serious problem—either in the relationship or with alcohol or both.* And, of course, no drugs for the same reasons. (Please note: When alcohol and/or drugs are a problem, professional help is advised.)

4. Other atmospherics (such as flowers, scented candles, etc.) are up to you.

5. Be sitting facing one another, knee-to-knee, eye-to-eye, and hand-in-hand if that is comfortable. You may be at a table, but be next to each other looking at one another and not at a distance across the table if at all possible. Definitely do not have this discussion in the nude or in bed or in the car.

6. Create as much comfort and safety as possible. Comfortable chairs, comfortable clothes, privacy and quiet are essential.

Once you have set the stage for your talk, you will want to acknowledge readiness, affirm your love for one another, and express appreciation and gratitude for the time you are about to spend together. You may wish to spend a moment holding hands or touching each other's arms or putting your hands on each other's laps. It's great to ask permission, especially if this sort of touch is not a usual part of your relationship dynamic. Be sure to look into each other's eyes. Join each other in taking three or four deep breaths. Whenever I am in this type of situation it is at this point I say to myself, "Arlen, *think love.*"

Exercise Two: Identifying the Elements of a Healthy Dialogue

Bobby and Charlie have done the hot button exercises and are ready to sit down to discuss what they've learned about themselves and how that relates to the problem they began to address in therapy. It is Friday night at 7:00, and they are getting ready for their conversation.

As they dialogue, see if you can pick up on how they set up the environment, use "I" messages, use mirroring, use "it's important to me" statements, identify hot buttons and incorporate the essential elements of a loving dialogue. Also note any "you" messages or times when a partner may use language that is less than loving. (See Appendix Three for my analysis of this discussion.)

> *Bobby:* Hey, Charlie, I'm ready for our talk. Do you feel ready to start?
>
> *Charlie:* I guess.
>
> *Bobby:* I'm feeling a little anxious.
>
> *Charlie:* Me, too. But I know we need to move into a better place with one another. I do love you, you know.
>
> *Bobby:* I love you, too, Charlie. And I appreciate your willingness to do this with me.

Charlie: Thank you. I appreciate you, and I want you to know that.

Bobby: So have you thought about where we should talk?

Charlie: I think the two big chairs in the den would work. Maybe we could move them so they face each other. Would that work for you?

Bobby: Perfect. I was thinking the same. I'd like to do a few candles and just have the lights on low in the room.

Charlie: That's fine. Music?

Bobby: Actually, I'd rather not. I'd like it to be really quiet, is that cool?

Charlie: Totally. I'll disconnect the phone. And we need to put away our cell phones.

Bobby: Done.

The couple set up the room and each take a seat. They are facing one another.

Bobby: Can we just hold hands for a couple of minutes?

Charlie: Sure.

Bobby: When I look into your eyes I see pain.

Charlie: I guess I feel upset that we have been arguing so much. I want things to be better.

Bobby: Well, that's why we're doing this. So, this is good. I feel upset, too, but it's going to be all right.

Charlie: Well, I think it would be good to talk first about our "hot buttons," don't you?

Bobby: Sure, we can do that. Who's going to go first?

Charlie: I will, if that's okay. I've really been giving this a lot of thought.

Bobby: Okay.

Charlie: Well, Bobby, as you know, my parents were always very overprotective. They needed to know everything I was doing. I remember, one time, a friend's mother paid for me and my friend to go on a carnival ride. When I told my mom about it she told me to never accept anything from anyone or go anywhere with anyone without asking her first—even though this was a friend who lived across the street, and our mothers were friends. My dad always would want me to go out and play ball with him, but I had no interest. So I realized, when I did that hot button exercise, that what I needed and wanted the most was to be allowed to choose to be with my own friends and do my own thing without being constantly watched and warned by my parents. And my last partner, Jim, was always on my case about where I was going and who I was with. I felt smothered and felt like he didn't trust me.

Bobby: So let me make sure I've got it. When you were a kid, your parents were overprotective and didn't let you choose your friends or your own interests. And, with Jim, you felt smothered and that he didn't trust you.

Charlie: Exactly. And so when you get upset about my going out with Tom it sets me off because it's like you're my mother. And it reminds me of Jim and how we ended things because of a lack of trust.

Bobby: Oh, wow, well that makes sense. I trust you…totally. And I want you to have your friends and do your own thing.

Charlie: Thank you.

Bobby: But I'd also like to come home after a hard day's work and find you home.

Charlie: Well, I'm not your puppy dog. I need my freedom.

Bobby: I didn't say you were. Now here we go. I can feel myself starting to get angry.

Charlie: Me, too. Me, too. Okay, I'm sorry about the "puppy dog" comment. We need to find a way to compromise about this issue. Why is it so important for me to be home when you get home if you trust me so much?

Bobby: Well, maybe this is a good time to talk about *my* hot buttons. When I was a kid we had a lot of family get-togethers. All the guys would be into throwing a ball around or playing touch football, and all the girls would be sitting around cooking and gossiping about the neighbors or other friends. I felt very left out and ignored. I'd end up playing some game alone, or reading a book off on the sidelines. And, in school, I wasn't into sports so I was always on the sidelines there, too. I remember watching the other boys playing and feeling very alone. So, when I come home and you're not here, I feel very alone. And knowing you're with someone else, even though I know it's not sexual or anything, I still feel left out.

Charlie: So, let me be sure I get this so I'm sure we're on the same page. Growing up, you felt alone and left out a lot, and so now when I'm not home you feel alone?

67

Bobby: Well, sorta. Let me see if I can make it a bit clearer. It's not that I feel alone. I feel left out when you're with someone else and I don't get to share that with you. I enjoy feeling connected... especially with you. So, when I come home, I like to feel that connection with you.

Charlie: Bobby, I can't be with you all the time.

Bobby: I didn't say you had to be with me all the time.

Charlie: You said you want me home when you get home, or you'll feel left out.

Bobby: Okay, okay, let me try again. I feel left out when I'm not included in activities that people I love are doing. I know I can't be with you all the time, but I also don't want to feel left out and disconnected. I understand that you need to have some independent space. I think we just need to find some way to balance the needs you have with the ones I have and compromise, like you said before.

Charlie: Bobby, I don't want you to feel left out or disconnected. I can understand why you're feeling that way because of how it was when you were a kid, and I feel bad about hitting your hot button there. I want to find a way to make you feel connected and still be able to have my own time.

Bobby: Well, thank you. I feel bad about seeming so possessive and getting on you about being out with Tom. I know you don't mean to leave me out. What kind of solution do you think we can come to?

Charlie: Would you feel better if I told you when I was going out without you?

Bobby: I felt this pang of pain when I heard "going out without you." Of course, I'd prefer you be home when I get home. For some reason, that is very important to me. At other times, it would be great if you'd just tell me.

Charlie: I feel a bit boxed in by having to always be home when you get home, but if it is really important to you I will try to do that. If I really can't be home then—or if I'm going to go out—I'll just let you know what I'm doing.

Bobby: May I ask a favor, then?

Charlie: Shoot.

Bobby: I feel really anxious asking this because I know it could push *your* hot button, but it's also pretty important to me. If you are going out with friends and you're not looking for a little space or time alone with them, could you invite me along? That would really help me to feel included, even if I don't go.

Charlie: I'll try to do that, too. Now may I ask you to do something for me?

Bobby: Okay?

Charlie: Thursday nights I like to go to happy hour with Tom. You usually come home during that time. I'd like to be able to have that one night out with my bud without feeling like I've done something wrong. I know it makes you feel left out, but I need a pal other than you to share private stuff with, you know? You know it's not the same as talking with you—you're my lover and my best friend. But you're not my "bud," you know. You're the one I'm in love with and want to be with every night. Tom is just the friend who has known me longer than anyone else in my life, and my private time with him is very important to me.

Bobby: I really get your need for private time with Tom, and I respect it. I think we've come to a good solution. I love you so much. I'm really glad we had this talk.

Charlie: Me, too. I love you, too, so much. I know we can make this work if we're honest with each other about our hot buttons.

Bobby: Thank you for sharing your feelings with me.

Charlie: You're the greatest!

Exercise Three: Hot Button Dialogue Rehearsal

Some people frown on the idea of rehearsing a conversation with your partner. It may seem to create a "script for discussion," rather than a heartfelt conversation. There is truth to this sentiment, but most people are going to need a bit of practice with the essential elements of a productive dialogue before talking directly to their partners about their hot buttons. Realize that the talk you imagine in advance will not be the same as the one you actually have with your partner.

However, it is *always* a good idea when you are anticipating your planned date to dialogue to: (1) give serious thought to your honest feelings, (2) determine where these feelings are coming from, (3) figure out the underlying beliefs you have associated with them, and (4) assess why your hot buttons are being pushed. You will be more able to enter the discussion with compassion and a realization that it's not all about you if you also: (1) contemplate how your partner might be feeling, (2) think about which of his hot buttons are being pushed, and (3) determine how to empathically connect with his past experiences and wounds. As well, it is totally okay to have an initial "I" statement prepared in your mind to make initiating conversation a bit easier.

In preparing for your date to dialogue to explain your hot buttons, you should take about 30 minutes or so to answer the following questions for yourself:

1. How will you ask your partner for a date to dialogue?

2. When the date arrives, how will you initiate a conversation about readiness?

3. What would you like to suggest to your partner to create an environment conducive to dialogue?

4. How might you affirm your love and gratitude for your partner? What are you truly grateful for in your relationship, and how will you express your appreciation?

5. Would you like there to be some initial physical touch? Do you believe your partner would feel comfortable with touch? How might you ask?

6. Assume, for this exercise, that you will initiate the conversation. Looking into your partner's eyes, what "I" statement would you like to make? What feeling(s) do you wish to express?

7. How will you explain your hot button(s) to your partner? What was missing or desired in childhood that you wish to share? What may have happened in past relationships to create sensitivity in you about certain issues? What underlying beliefs contribute to your vulnerability?

8. How might you ask your partner if he is ready to share his hot button(s) with you?

9. Assume for this exercise that your partner does open up to you. Imagine how his history and experience might create sensitivity and vulnerability. How might you use empathy, compassion, reassurance, appreciation, compromise and validation to let him know you love him and understand?

10. What might be a loving way to end the conversation and be sure both of you feel complete?

Exercise Four: The Real Thing

Once you have completed Exercise Three, it is time to have the real hot button dialogue with your partner. Put the exercise away, and go into the date to dialogue with an open heart and an open mind. Bring no expectations into the conversation. Be curious about how it will unfold, knowing you are about to take your relationship to a new level. Don't assume you know what your partner will say. Rather than listening to your partner with your next response in mind, *listen* to your partner with empathic understanding in mind. Any intimate dialogue can be anxiety provoking, so if you need to, tell your partner, "I feel anxious." And remember to say to yourself, "Think love."

Upon completion of your dialogue, when you have a chance to spend thirty minutes or so alone, answer—for yourself—the following questions:

1. Did the conversation surprise you in any way? If so, how?

2. Were you able to relate your hot buttons, your underlying beliefs, your childhood wounds and past hurts, needs and desires to your partner? If so, how did it feel? If not, why not? What blocked the energy? How might you try again?

3. Did you learn anything new from your partner? Do you understand where he is coming from? What are his hot buttons and what created them?

4. How well did you show empathy? Did you feel compassion? Did you express appreciation? Were you able to reassure and validate your partner's feelings?

5. Did you feel complete when you were done? Is there anything you wish you had said—or had not said? Is there anything your partner said that stirred some emotions that you did not resolve? Did you address compromise? How might you ask for another date to dialogue to address any unresolved feelings or issues?

We discussed, in Chapter Two, the need to honestly discuss sexual issues as they arise in our relationships. Among the toughest topics to address is the loss of desire for our partner. In fact, the number one reason couples come to me for sex therapy is loss of desire. It is not unusual to see that the loss of desire is related to a sexual template issue. So, how do you tell your partner that he has fallen out of your template? I would suggest the use of "I" messages after a full explanation and discussion of sexual templates. *When you thoroughly understand the sexual template, you realize that the loss of desire is not intentional.*

People do not choose to lose interest in their partners. However, if there is something that can be done to reverse the problem, why not try it? I gave the example in Chapter Two of hair length and weight as resolvable template issues. What if you were to say to your partner, after explaining sexual templates, "You know, when we met you had the sexiest beard and were so nice and trim. Those things really turned me on to you. I feel really weird and a bit shallow saying this, but I think if you grew your beard back and lost some weight it would help me feel more sexually attracted to you."

> *When you thoroughly understand the sexual template, you realize that the loss of desire is not intentional.*

A discussion is much more sensitive when the sexual template issue is not correctable. For example, the man who erotically desires only young men will have a sexual problem in his relationship as his partner ages. (This, by the way, is not an unusual problem.) We will explore options for dealing with waning desire or irresolvable loss of desire in Part Two and Part Three of this book. Once you understand your options you will be better prepared to have a dialogue about the challenge. But, you *must* talk about levels of desire, passion, and satisfaction with your sex life in order to preserve intimacy in your relationship.

Gay men today, more frequently than ever before, find themselves in discussions about marriage and children. Jamie, a client in his early forties, came to me after proposing marriage to Tony, his partner of nine years. He told me that Tony agreed, but Jamie expressed disappointment because Tony didn't seem to have much passion or enthusiasm about tying the knot. After talking with Jamie for a while, I learned that Tony was going through a tough time at work with a new boss, and his job security at the company was "iffy." I suggested that Jamie have a conversation with his partner, and express his feelings with "I" messages to see if the marriage idea would be best left for a more stable period in Tony's life. Jamie went home and did just that:

> *Jamie:* You know, Tony, I'm feeling disappointed about our conversation about marriage the other day. I'm wondering if you really are okay with the idea.

> *Tony:* I thought we agreed we would do it.

> *Jamie:* Yeah, but I'm sensing your heart is not in it. I felt a little bad after thinking about it some because I realized it might not be the best time for you with all that's going on at work.

> *Tony:* Well, work is very stressful right now, but, really, I'm more concerned about how my mother

and grandparents will take it. You know they are just getting comfortable with the idea of my being gay and living with you. Throwing marriage in their faces may be over the top for them.

By using "I" statements to address the issue directly, Jamie found out what was actually going on with Tony. Unless we talk to our partners about our feelings, we are likely to fantasize about what is going on in their heads without really knowing the truth. It does not matter how long a couple has been together, people are not mind readers, and without asking we are making assumptions. With this new information, Jamie can have an ongoing discussion with Tony about his true feelings, and the couple can decide together about marriage. Tony, then, is not just going along with Jamie to avoid conflict, which may have led to discomfort, at best, and resentment, at worst. At the same time, Jamie can begin to assess for himself how important the marriage question is in light of Tony's concern, as well as being sensitive to the external stressors that play into such a decision.

Exercise Five: Resolving Your Relationship Conflict

Most of the difficult situations causing conflict with our partners can be traced back to our hot buttons.

It is now time to try out all you've learned in this chapter. Think about a recent incident, situation or feeling that came up for you in your relationship that created conflict, tension or pain. You are now going to deal with it with your partner. Remember: *Most of the difficult situations causing conflict with our partners can be traced back to our hot buttons.* You now know what your hot buttons are and what your partner's hot buttons are, as well. Take some time to think about the situation, how it impacted you emotionally (i.e., what feelings came up), what hot buttons were pushed, which ones were pushed for your partner and what underlying beliefs and life experiences may have been the root causes. Make a date to dialogue, suggesting a discussion about the recent incident that has caused some conflict, tension or pain.

In thinking about your upcoming dialogue, consider:

1. When the date arrives, how will you initiate a conversation about readiness?

2. What would you like to suggest to your partner to create an environment conducive to dialogue?

3. How might you affirm your love and gratitude for your partner? What are you truly grateful for in your relationship, and how will you express your appreciation?

4. Would you like there to be some initial physical touch? Do you believe your partner would feel comfortable with touch? How might you ask?

5. Assume, for this exercise, that you will initiate the conversation. Looking into your partner's eyes, what "I" statement would you like to make? What feeling(s) do you wish to express?

6. How will you explain what hot button(s) were activated by the recent occurrence? What was missing or desired in childhood that may have contributed to your emotional reaction? What may have happened in past relationships to create sensitivity in you about certain issues? What underlying beliefs contributed to your vulnerability?

7. How might you ask your partner to share his perspective?

8. Assuming your partner does open up to you, imagine how his history and experiences might have caused his sensitivity and vulnerability. How will you use

empathy, compassion, reassurance and validation to let him know you love him and understand?

9. What compromise(s) might create mutual understanding and satisfaction? What might be a loving way to end the conversation and be sure each of you feel complete?

You may or may not wish to write down the answers to the questions posed above, but *do not* take any written material—including this book—into the dialogue environment. Come at this from your heart; don't be afraid to express how you feel about having the conversation in this moment, and *think love*.

Upon completion of your dialogue, when you have a chance to spend thirty minutes or so alone, answer for yourself the following questions:

1. Did the conversation surprise you in any way? If so, how?

2. Were you able to relate the situation to your hot buttons, your underlying beliefs, your childhood wounds and past hurts, needs and desires, and communicate them effectively to your partner? If so, how did it feel? If not, why not? What blocked the energy? How might you try again?

3. Did you learn anything new from your partner? Do you understand where he is coming from in this matter? What are his hot buttons and what created them?

4. How well did you show empathy? Did you feel compassion? Were you able to reassure and validate your partner's feelings?

5. Did you feel complete when you were done? Is there anything you wish you had said or had not said? Is there anything your partner said that stirred some

emotions that you did not resolve? Were you able to reach a compromise? How might you ask for another date to dialogue to address any unresolved feelings or issues?

The process of addressing conflict, tension and pain by creating vulnerability and expressing feelings inevitably results in the creation of greater intimacy.

A couple with sexual issues must first meet the challenge of learning to create vulnerability and dialogue about tough issues before attempting to conquer sexual problems.

It takes courage to have open and honest conversations with you partner. It will take courage to do the sexual enhancement work in the next section of the book. It is no coincidence that "courage" comes from the Latin word "cor," meaning heart. *Opening the heart and moving into your fear is the necessary risk required for true intimacy. Don't be afraid to be afraid. Feel the fear, feel the feelings and express them to your partner.*

As you complete this chapter, you now have the basic tools to communicate more effectively. You may even have already found a new physical openness and connection with your partner as a result of the exercises you have worked through with him. Whether or not you've already improved upon your sexual connection, if you have begun to feel some comfort and safety by lovingly addressing the conflict, tension and pain in your relationship, then you and your partner are ready to take the next step.

Let's move into the bedroom.

Opening the heart and moving into your fear is the necessary risk required for true intimacy. Don't be afraid to be afraid. Feel the fear, feel the feelings and express them to your partner.

PART TWO

Creative Sexual Enhancement

Chapter Four

Sexual Desire vs. Sexual Disorder

You are likely reading this book because you want to improve the sexual intimacy in your life. We have, thus far, discussed how passionate sexual relationships evolve and dissolve and how communication is critical for intimacy and sexual connection. As you continue reading, Part Two will guide you through exercises and experiential exploration for sexual enhancement. However, before we start on that journey it is necessary to rule out true sexual disorders as the cause of failed sexual interaction with your partner.

The primary reason I see couples for sex therapy is a disparity in levels of sexual desire. The partner with the "problem" or "identified patient," tends to be the partner with lesser desire, and we will spend some time in this chapter looking at possible causes for that lack of desire. But, sometimes the partner with more desire— or desire for sex outside of the relationship—is accused of being a "sex addict" by his partner, or has actually been diagnosed with sex addiction by his therapist. Let's take a moment to discuss the concept of sex addiction and compulsion.

Hypersexuality

Sexologists are not in complete agreement as to what sex addiction is—or if it even exists. Many who adopt a diagnosis of "sex addiction" will state that, physiologically, the brain of a sex addict generates the same neurochemicals that drug and alcohol addiction produces—leading people to engage in excessive behavior. The effect of this is an inability to contain or control the addictive behavior, resulting in the destruction of normal life functioning. However, there are other sexologists who feel the term "addiction" is misleading. They believe that, unlike alcohol or drugs, sex is a normal biological function—it does not produce physical withdrawal symptoms when the behavior is curtailed—and norms for sexual activity are standardized by the particular culture and society and are not universal.

The *Diagnostic and Statistical Manual of Mental Disorders* (DSM) published by the American Psychiatric Association (APA), does not cite sexual addiction as an actual diagnosis. The APA has proposed a possible new diagnosis of "Hypersexual Disorder," relegated to the DSM appendix, for consideration by the mental health community. Hypersexual disorder would consist of multiple criteria to include significant personal distress or impairment to life functioning as a result of sexual thoughts and/or activity. It appears psychiatrists and sexologists face a considerable challenge in agreeing on set criteria for a definitive diagnosis of Hypersexual Disorder.

Without agreed-upon criteria, it is important for sexologists and therapists to avoid labeling any repetitive sexual behaviors or fantasies based on their own personal ideas of what is considered "normal" sexual activity or desire. For example, a man having sex twice a day with different sexual partners through the week is frequently considered sex addicted, but a man having sex with his partner twice a day is not. The conclusion is that frequency, in and of itself, is a flawed diagnostic criterion.

Most sexologists agree that it is essential to focus on how repetitive sexual thoughts or activity actually impact a man's life and his possible reasons for acting out sexually. Multiple factors are likely to be at play when sexual obsession and compulsion adversely affect a man's relationships, work and other life activities. Sexually compulsive men may use sex to reduce anxiety-laden thoughts; to avoid conflict and confrontation; to avoid emotional pain, hurt and fear; or to distract from life's disappointments. The underlying etiology is best diagnosed and explored in psychotherapy. Psychotherapeutic intervention, then, is a critical first step if you want to reestablish a good sexual connection with your partner when there is repetitive sexual behavior happening, which is either resulting in the disruption of daily life activities or negatively impacting relational intimacy.

If one or both partners want to experience sex outside the relationship, that is not in-and-of-itself sexual addiction, compulsion or hypersexual disorder.

A most significant point, however, is that if both partners in a relationship want and enjoy sex together—but one wants more sex than the other—that is not in-and-of-itself sexual addiction, compulsion or hypersexual disorder. *If one or both partners want to experience sex outside the relationship, that is not in-and-of-itself sexual addiction, compulsion or hypersexual disorder.* We refer to addiction, compulsion or hypersexual disorder *only* when there is disruption and/or unmanageability of daily life, leading to more pain than pleasure. However, if disparity in sexual desire is the problem, the couple needs to make a date to dialogue and use the communication tools, found in Chapter Three of this book, to find solutions.

Hypoactive Sexual Desire

As previously stated, the number one problem couples bring into my practice is declining or absent sexual desire. It is necessary to distinguish between a loss of desire for your partner and a generalized loss of sexual desire. You may be able to establish this for yourself by asking yourself the following questions:

1. Do I see men on a daily basis that create sexual interest for me?

2. Do I fantasize about having sex with men other than my partner?

3. Do I want to masturbate or actually masturbate thinking about other men?

4. Do I have or want to have sex with men other than my partner?

If the answer to any of these questions is "yes," you can be pretty sure the lack of sexual desire is directed at your partner and not generalized to all men. If the answer to all of them is "no," and you find your libido (sex drive) is low, then you are looking at a hypoactive sexual desire disorder. The cause of the problem may be biological and/ or psychological.

The first step in treating this disorder is to rule out any physical problems by seeing a physician. You will want to have a complete physical, with blood work—including testosterone and estrogen levels. (Your hormones play an extremely significant role in the strength of your libido and your sense of well-being. I even recommend a hormonal evaluation for men who are depressed. As is the case with libido problems, often a depressed mood can be lifted with testosterone supplementation.) Other medical problems and medications can also interfere with normal sexual appetite and functioning. These include, but are not limited to, diabetes, heart disease, depression, anxiety, alcohol, recreational drugs, medications for high blood pressure and medications for depression. If you are experiencing diminished libido and taking medications, ask your physician about any possible sexual side effects and if alternative medications are available.

Aging also plays a prominent role in sexual appetite and function. While most men slow down sexually with age, it is a myth to think that sex has to stop at some point in the life cycle. As the saying goes, "I may be old, but I'm not dead yet!" Again, often hormonal supplementation may be rejuvenating, but know that it is okay to slow down and enjoy sex and sensual intimacy within the parameters of your physical health and stamina.

It is important to accept and feel good about your body in order to share and enjoy it with your partner.

Psychological factors affecting desire include, but are not limited to, self-acceptance and body image. We touched upon this in Chapter One, and we will have an exercise in the next chapter to explore body image. *It is important to accept and feel good about your body in order to share and enjoy it with your partner.* As well, feeling bad about being gay or feeling as though gay sex and relationships are not valuable or viable can adversely affect your desire to engage sexually with another man.

Another potential problem is Sexual Aversion Disorder, which is defined as disgust about sex or sexual contact and activity. This also may be associated with negative feelings about gay sexual activity, and it is often related to deep-seated processes rooted in family dynamics and/or sexual abuse as a child. It is extremely important to get professional help when there is any history of sexual, emotional or physical trauma, as it can be devastating to mature sexual relationships and intimacy.

Orgasmic Disorders

There are basically two disorders affecting ejaculation—inhibited male orgasm, and premature or "rapid" ejaculation. Inhibited orgasm (delayed or absent orgasm) requires professional medical assessment before you attempt to evaluate and treat any psychological factors. Included in such an assessment would be: (1) conditions or treatments such as removal of a cancerous prostate gland resulting in retrograde ejaculation (semen backing up into the bladder rather than ejaculating down the urethra); (2) the effects of drugs, medication or alcohol; and (3) age. Psychotherapy may be necessary to work through mental health factors, such as lack of self-acceptance and prior traumatic experiences.

Premature or rapid ejaculation can be a difficult problem for couples, as well. Often defined as orgasmic release before one wishes to ejaculate, its manifestation may vary considerably. Professional assessment must, once again, look at factors such as: (1) age; (2) desire for one's partner; (3) frequency of ejaculation; and (4) the effects of drugs, medication or alcohol. Treatment options vary, and a sex therapist is your best resource for dealing with ejaculatory disorders.

Erectile Disorder

You cannot pick up a magazine or watch a television show today without some advertisement for so-called "E.D." treatment. Erectile disorder is often called "erectile dysfunction" or "impotence" and is the most common sexual issue for men. The terms dysfunction and impotence inadvertently—and often *inaccurately*—contribute to a man's feeling of powerless over his erection. As with most of the sexual disorders, the inability to attain or maintain an erection (or a complete erection) may result from biological and/or psychological causes. A medical evaluation is the critical first step in diagnosing the causes. Drugs, medication and alcohol are very frequently the cause of erectile problems. Diseases such as diabetes and coronary artery disease are also associated with erectile disorder. As we age, the firmness of the erection decreases, and the time it takes to achieve erection increases. However, a primary cause of erectile disorder is performance anxiety, not uncommonly related to lack of erotic desire for your partner.

Viagra, Cialis and Levitra are some of the effective prescription medications for Erectile Disorder, but they are not aphrodisiacs and they do not produce desire. Trying to overcome desire-based challenges with one of these medications will not work. There are other treatments, including penile implants and injections into the penis that are available for working with E.D. originating from medically related conditions. Vacuum aspirators (pumps) and venous retention rings (cock rings) offer varying degrees of success for E.D., as well.

When the underlying cause of E.D. is psychological, a cognitive-behavioral sex therapy approach typically works best. E.D., as well as the orgasmic disorders, is often rapidly cured by using the mind to redirect the focus of attention. A man who ejaculates prematurely does well to direct his focus *away from* the object of his erotic desire. A man who has difficulty achieving erection or ejaculation does well to direct his focus *toward* the object of his erotic desire. (The next two chapters will address how shifting your focus can be achieved even when you lack sexual desire for your partner.)

Performance anxiety—one of the major causes of E.D.—is essentially a misdirected focus of attention on matters other than an object of sexual desire. When you are concerned about your ability to satisfy your partner, are

> *Viagra, Cialis and Levitra are some of the effective prescription medications for Erectile Disorder, but they are not aphrodisiacs and they do not produce desire.*

self-conscious about your body, or are thinking about some problem at work, you are not focused on the sexual stimulus—the partner or fantasy in your mind. Similarly, when you move out of the moment of sexual connection and pleasure you are no longer focused on the sexual stimulus. Redirection is necessary in order to be sexual. One of the most enjoyable aspects of sex can be losing yourself in the moment with your partner. Worry, anxiety, concern and fear take you out of the here-and-now of sexual experience.

Diagnosing and treating sexual problems is best accomplished by licensed professionals. Working alongside your physician and (sex) therapist, your diagnosis and treatment can be most effectively accomplished. Because sexual challenges are multifaceted and may include medical, biological, psychological and/or social factors, they are often not a simple matter to address. Remember: This book is *not* a substitute for professional attention. The exercises and experiential suggestions are meant to be used by couples who have ruled out and received appropriate care for any and all underlying physical and mental health problems.

> *Diagnosing and treating sexual problems is best accomplished by licensed professionals.*

Questions to Ponder:

1. Has there been disparity in the sexual desire you and your partner have for one another? What are some possible causes? If you have not discussed the disparity, how might you begin a dialogue? What would be your objective(s)?

2. If you experience a lack of sexual appetite, do you recognize it as a generalized lack of desire or is it specifically directed toward your partner? How might you best discuss the issue with your partner?

3. Are you challenged by repetitive sexual thoughts or activities that are all-consuming, thereby adversely impacting your work, your relationships or your usual

life activities? If so, what has prevented you from seeking professional care?

4. Do you find aging or age disparity impacting the sexual intimacy in your relationship or in your life? What possible solutions might you discuss with your partner? What steps would you like to take to meet these challenges?

5. Are you aware of any sexual disorder you have, which is creating issues with physical intimacy? What steps could you take to attempt to remedy that?

Chapter Five

The Sensual Journey: Seven Exercises for Creative Intimacy

You are about to engage in a series of experiential exercises focused on enhancing the sexual connection and intimacy between you and your partner. The journey ahead has no particular destination as every couple has a unique experience. In fact, the concept of "beginner's mind" is particularly apropos as you move through these exercises. In other words, have no expectations and meet the challenges as a beginner might—with curiosity and an open heart and mind.

In the 1970s, pioneering sexologists William Masters and Virginia Johnson, a married couple, developed a groundbreaking technique for heterosexual couples with sexual challenges. Introduced in their book *Human Sexual Inadequacy* "sensate focus" has, since, been the foundation of clinical sex therapy. By focusing on the sensations of physical touch without an expectation for sex or orgasm, Masters and Johnson found couples were free from any anxiety around performance and could engage their true feelings.

In the 1980s, Dagmar O'Connor, a student of Masters and Johnson, expanded on sensate focus in her book *How To*

Make Love To The Same Person For The Rest Of Your Life And Still Love It and developed workshops with ~~exercises~~ ~~for marriage enhancement.~~ In the early 2000s, I, myself, set out to expand upon the work of earlier sexologists with a concentration on enhancing the sexual connection for gay men. I wrote *Sexual Enhancement Therapy for Gay Men in Long Term Relationships* for my PhD dissertation.

The exercises in the following chapter are a modification of my work designed for a self-guided experience in sensate focus for gay male couples. *It is ideally recommended that these exercises be supervised by a licensed and certified sex therapist.* I want to warn you, before you engage in the prescribed activities, that feelings and issues may arise that could necessitate seeking professional help. If you are already working with a therapist, be sure to get his or her input before moving into this work. And, as previously mentioned, if there is any history of abuse or sexual trauma, you *must* have professional attention and guidance prior to and during these sensate focus and sexual exercises.

> ~
>
> *It is ideally recommended that these exercises be supervised by a licensed and certified sex therapist.*
>
> ~

The experience ahead is a step by-step exploration of yourself and of your partner's sexual interests and desires with the intended outcome of creatively enhancing your intimate connection. You may, at times, feel the guided exercises are too directive, authoritarian and scripted. I will agree that they are all that, but there is a method to the madness. Have patience with the process and allow it to unfold at a comfortable pace. It takes courage (heart) to do these exercises as you will create considerable vulnerability, with no certainty of the outcomes. However, keep in mind that increased vulnerability results in increased intimacy. Stay in the moment without expectation and be present with your partner. After all, you are riding this wave together; you are a united team in this adventure.

Each exercise begins with a purpose, but no direction for a specific end result. Pay attention to this purpose as you read the instructions. Once you and your partner have read through the exercise together and understand the format and intention, put the book away and go to the bedroom. You do not want the experience to feel like you are acting out a recipe from a cookbook. The written instructions are merely a guide to achieving the specified purpose.

Creating the supportive environment as you did with the dialogues in Chapter Three is necessary before starting any of the exercises in this chapter. The necessary supportive elements for sensate focus include:

1. Have enough light to be able to see into each other's eyes and sense facial expressions, but not too much light as to be glaring. You may use candlelight, flowers, incense and other atmospherics to enhance a romantic mood.

2. Have no distractions…none. No TV, no (cell) phone, no computer. Soft background music is fine.

3. Do not eat during these exercises. Do not drink alcohol or use recreational drugs before, during or immediately after the exercises.

4. Keep the room temperature slightly warmer than usual for your comfort while undressed.

5. Acknowledge readiness and confirm who will be going first as explained in each exercise. Affirm your love for one another and express appreciation and gratitude while looking into each other's eyes. Taking one another's hands or engaging in a hug or light touch before getting into bed is also highly reassuring and affirming.

6. Take three or four deep breaths together.

7. Think love.

At the end of each exercise there is a series of "Questions to Ponder" with your partner. The dialogue created by answering these questions is at the heart of enhancing your physical and emotional connection. Be sure to use the communication skills you developed in Chapter Three to guide your conversation.

If your relationship is working well sexually, these exercises may not be necessary, but may help bring more sensuality and intimacy into your love life. If your sexual relationship is not working as well as you may like, but there is still a sexual connection, the exercises may well enhance that connection. If you and your partner are disconnected sexually, the exercises may or may not create a sexual reconnection, but more than likely they will increase your level of intimate connection. The key point here is that *every couple is different and unique, and all outcomes are different and unique.* No particular outcome is right or wrong, good or bad. Always remember the focus is on observation and a sense of presence in the moment with your partner. No matter the nature of the experience, these exercises will surely enhance honest communication about sensuality, sex and sexual feelings. Nearly all of the men I have worked with report that the exercises brought them closer and helped them to communicate better—both in and out of the bedroom.

> *…every couple is different and unique, and all outcomes are different and unique.*

Exercise One: Focus on Touch

The purpose of this exercise is to give and receive non-genital touch without sex and to focus on the sensations of touching and being touched. You need to plan for two thirty- to forty-five-minute sessions so each partner may experience touch as both a giver and as a receiver. You do not have to do the exercises back-to-back, and most couples choose to take a break, or even a "day off," between giving and receiving. The giver will be in control in this exercise, and a coin toss before you begin will determine who is giver first. Create the supportive environment in your bedroom and affirm readiness, love and appreciation before you begin.

Start the exercise by getting undressed. If as a couple you have never had sex, have never been undressed in each other's presence or for some other reason do not feel comfortable at this time undressing for your partner, you may leave your undergarments on and repeat the exercise once or twice a week until you feel you can proceed without clothes.

The partner to receive touch first lies down on the bed, face down, turning over on his back half way through the thirty- to forty-five-minute encounter. The giver is now instructed to take his time and touch his partner wherever he likes, while *avoiding* the receiver's nipples, buttocks, perineum (the area between your scrotum and anus) and genitals. The giver may touch, rub, massage, stroke, caress or simply hold an area of his partner's body, utilizing varying degrees of pressure over varying lengths of the body. However, do not think of this as "giving my partner a massage." The object is to experience touch in many different ways, while being creative and loving in the process. The giver may use massage oil, lotions or powders. Talcum powder, baby powder or cornstarch may be lightly sprinkled on an area of your partner's body before stroking. Utilize body lubricants sparingly, and for the sole purpose of reducing any friction from dry, rough or chapped hands.

The giver makes decisions about lighting, candles, incense and other romantic atmospherics with the approval of his partner, but the lights are to remain on throughout the exercise. The temperature in the room should be adjusted by the giver with particular attention to the comfort of the receiver.

The receiver is to focus on the sensations he experiences. The giver, likewise, is to experience the sensations of touching and, at the same time, pay attention to which sensations the receiver likes and dislikes.

The receiver should guide the giver verbally—and nonverbally—by telling his partner what areas of the

SEX HAPPENS

body, what kinds of touch and pressure, and what lotions
or powders he finds unpleasant or particularly pleasant.
It is best to use sentences starting with the word "I" to
communicate your feelings. For example, "I actually like
lighter touch on my shoulder" or "I would prefer having my
neck rubbed" or "I don't really enjoy being touched under
my arm." Be careful not to scold or criticize your partner
with harsh comments that start with the word "you," such
as, "You know I'm ticklish. Don't touch me over there!"
Be gentle with one another, as this can be a difficult and
emotional process.

The receiver may also put his hand over the giver's hand and
gently direct the movement away from displeasure and/
or toward more pleasurable areas. Guiding pressure and
movement is fine, remembering that the giver is focusing
on *his own* desires in terms of where and how he wants
to touch his partner. *Asking for, or showing, your partner
what feels good or not so good is a necessary part of a loving
sexual relationship.*

Although the giver is exploring his own interest while
touching and feeling, he needs, first and foremost, to
be committed to avoiding areas of discomfort for his
partner. As you go through this exercise you will want to
relax, breathe deeply and be present in the moment with
your partner. It is acceptable to close your eyes during
this exercise.

When the giver determines by the clock that the exercise
time is complete, you should spend a few minutes lying in
bed together. Avoid the urge to discuss the experience at
this point, but *acknowledging love* at this moment can be
extremely comforting.

> *Asking for, or showing, your partner what feels good or not so good is a necessary part of a loving sexual relationship.*

THE SENSUAL JOURNEY

Ten important guidelines as you do this exercise:

1. Stay with the _sensual_. This is not a sexual exercise.

2. Do everything _slowly_, so you have time to feel everything both physically and emotionally.

3. All feelings are _okay_, even sadness, boredom or anger should they arise. Allow yourself the full range of emotional experience.

4. Have _no_ expectations. Stay in the moment with your partner.

5. If you get aroused sexually—or _don't_ get aroused—it makes no difference.

6. Take care of yourself. Focus on your own sense of well-being and the sensations that arise. Take responsibility for your own comfort. Let go of everything that is not about the touch you are experiencing, both as giver and receiver.

7. For this exercise do _not_ kiss.

8. Do _not_ use alcohol or drugs before, during or immediately after the exercise.

9. Do _not_ touch your own body during the exercise.

10. _No matter what comes up, do not have sex with your partner or masturbate during or immediately following this exercise!_

After _both_ partners have had an opportunity to give and receive in this exercise, make a date to dialogue to discuss what the experience was like for you and discuss the feelings that came up. Review the following Questions to Ponder in preparation for your dialogue.

Questions to Ponder:

1. How did it *feel* to be a giver! How did it *feel* to be a receiver? Use the Inventory of Feelings (Appendix Two) to tap into the full range of your emotional experience. What communication skills will you use to share these feelings with your partner?

2. Were you able to let go of expectations? How did it feel to be free from any obligation to figure out how to please your partner?

3. Did anything surprise you during this exercise? Did you learn anything new about your partner, your partner's body, or what he likes or dislikes? Did you learn anything new about yourself, your body, or what you might like or dislike? Discuss any new discoveries and how you might use these insights to improve your connection with your partner.

4. Did you prefer to give or receive? How does that match up with the giving and receiving dynamic in your day-to-day life with your partner? If there is a discrepancy in desire, did you find that the partner with more desire for his mate was more into giving than his partner? Was the partner with less desire more into receiving than giving? How might you discuss these differences with your partner?

5. How did you communicate your needs during this exercise? Were you able to take responsibility for your own comfort and sense of well-being? Did you ever feel you were not in control? If yes, why? Did you ever avoid expressing any unpleasant feelings to protect your partner's feelings?

6. Did you ever feel emotionally uncomfortable? Did you relate this to your partner? If not, why not? If yes, were you able to express yourself gently and completely?

7. Were you ever bored or distracted? Were there times you were unable to be thoroughly involved in the process and connected with your partner? If so, why do you suppose you moved out of the moment? What barriers or blocks were revealed that may be standing in the way of a greater physical connection with your partner? Were there any sexual template issues triggered during the exercise that moved you out of the moment? If yes, did you discover what may be keeping you from a greater physical connection with your partner? How will you discuss these with your partner?

8. Did any memories come up that took you out of the moment? Any from childhood or previous relationships? Any from your current relationship with your partner? Were they disturbing? Were they pleasant? How will you discuss these with your partner?

9. Did any future concerns come up that took you out of the moment? Were they anxiety-provoking? Do you sense that they might adversely affect your relationship? How might you explore these with your partner?

10. Were you ever sexually aroused during the exercise as giver or receiver? Was your partner ever aroused? If one of you was aroused but not the other, how did that feel? Did you find yourself concerned about any difference in experience? If you were aroused, how did it feel to be aroused without satisfying the urge to be sexual? How will you discuss this with your partner?

11. Did you ever feel great joy during the process? Be sure to share this with your partner.

12. Do you feel closer to our partner now? If so, share your feelings about this closeness with your partner.

Your dialogue should follow the same guidelines for creating a supportive environment, affirming readiness, love and appreciation as you did in Chapter Three. In preparation for your date to dialogue, be sure to review the essentials of a loving dialogue. Be certain to give consideration to any hot buttons that may have been triggered as a result of the exercise. Be as honest, direct and complete in answering the questions and fully expressing your feelings—both positive and negative.

Unlike the other dialogues, you will want to take this book into the dialogue with you so all of the questions are addressed, but do *not* have your answers written down. You should have given thought to the questions, but you will want this discussion to be from the heart as it unfolds in the moment. Have no expectations. Approach the dialogue with an openness to learn new things about your partner, yourself, and your relationship. *Think love.*

Give yourself some time after the discussion to evaluate your feelings and thoughts. Use the following Questions to Ponder to assist you in the introspective process.

Questions to Ponder After Exercise Dialogues:

1. How do you feel about the dialogue with your partner? Do you feel both of you were open about the experience and resultant feelings?

2. What did your partner share with you that was surprising? What, if anything, did he have to say that upset you? Did either of you push the other's hot buttons? If so, how did you talk through the underlying beliefs and past experiences that triggered those hot buttons? How did you express your emotional reactions to his disclosures?

3. If possible, how do you think you might be able to improve on your sensual connection with your partner after this discussion?

4. If there were any sexual template issues, how were they addressed and how did you feel about the conversation?

5. Did you feel complete when you finished talking? Do you need another date to dialogue for closure? What, if anything, do you still need to express to your partner? Would professional counseling be beneficial?

6. Do you feel closer to your partner after the exercise and dialogue? Did you feel an increased vulnerability? If so, was there a resultant increase in intimacy? Whether small or large, did you and your partner discuss any shift in feelings for one another as a result of the exercise? If so, how does it leave you feeling now? If not, how might you address it now?

There are as many possible outcomes for Exercise One as there are men who complete the exercise. My work with men has uncovered six basic experiences. See if you and your partner are able to identify with one of the following generalized couple types.

Basic Outcomes for Exercise One

Couple Type #1

Both partners felt good about the experience. There were no real surprises, and both partners acknowledged that they know each other's touch well as a result of the time they've been together. While the experience felt good, there was no sexual arousal, which seemed okay for the couple. The partners enjoyed the exercise, were relaxed and able to stay in the moment most of the time. There were no control issues and nothing really surfaced from the past.

This couple type usually has a waning or absent sexual connection, but are emotionally well connected. The partners here generally feel a bit closer after the experience.

There may be some sexual template match problems, but they are less important to this couple than the closeness they experience with mutual touch. Continued work may improve their sexual connection, but they know after Exercise One that they can engage in touch and feel nicely connected. In my practice, I might recommend repeating the exercise once before going on to Exercise Two, but the couple does well to keep the exercise in mind for future intimate, if not sexual, time together.

Couple Type #2

Both partners feel great about the experience. The format released any pressure to perform. There were some new discoveries about each other. There was some mutual sexual arousal which they enjoyed, but they did not engage sexually. One or the other, or both, partners reported some difficulty in not taking the experience into the realm of sex play. There were no control issues and nothing surfaced from the past.

This couple type often has a waning or intermittent sexual connection and is emotionally connected. These partners definitely feel closer and have more optimism about sexual intimacy after Exercise One. The continued exercises will most likely enhance their sexual connection, and I would recommend going right on to Exercise Two.

Couple Type #3

Both partners got totally into the exercise, became very sexually aroused and engaged in sex. These partners stayed in the moment without issues of control or problems from the past. They may be seeking help because they have a high-conflict relationship or circumstantial situations of life at this time have interfered with the regularity or intensity of their sexual connection. The exercise helped them engage their love for one another sexually. The couple is feeling closer as a result of the experience.

I often recommend this couple work on setting limits with one another. I may ask them to repeat the exercise *without* sex before going on to Exercise Two. If they set up an expectation for sex with each exercise, they will inadvertently create pressure to have sex with each experience. The expectation could actually diminish growing sexual energy and lead to disappointment and discouragement.

Couple Type #4

One partner enjoyed the exercise and one did not. Often the dissatisfied partner is having a sexual template issue with his partner, and no longer desires him or enjoys touching him. He may enjoy being touched, but there was insufficient sexual attraction and passion to enjoy the giving part of the experience, and he found himself bored at times during the exercise. There may have been sexual arousal for the man who is enjoying—and is desirous of—his partner, and the disparity may be uncomfortable and difficult for the couple to discuss. They may be doing these exercises because they are hoping to reverse a long-standing decline in their physical relationship.

Couple Type #4 is the type of couple I see most often in my sexology practice. The prognosis for reigniting the sexual passion for the dissatisfied partner is dependent, to a large degree, on how much passion there was in the beginning of the relationship, how much passion is left today, how long they have gone without sex, how well this couple can communicate about their feelings, and whether there is anything the one partner can do to reenter the other's sexual template. This couple is encouraged to repeat Exercise One and, during the dialogue, specifically focus on discussing how the sexual template match is suffering. We may find that, with honest and open conversation and continuing work on sensate focus, some sexual feelings may emerge. I also encourage the partner lacking desire to focus on those attributes in his partner that do evoke

erotic desire or once did, as well as fantasize about his
partner's desirable characteristics as he re~~ally them from~~
~~an earlier time~~ in their relationship. (We will address
seduction and fantasy further with other exercises, and
in Chapter Six. Until then, I suggest the couple engage
their emotional connection through touch during
these exercises.)

Couple Type #5

Neither partner could honestly get into the exercise.
Both found it difficult to give, and often one or both
found it difficult to receive. There were no real surprises,
and frequently both partners were rather bored with the
exercise. They may or may not have found it gratifying
being with one another undressed and in bed, but mostly
there was no real enjoyment and no arousal for either
partner. This couple may never have had a strong sexual
connection and likely have not had a physical relationship
in quite some time.

There are basically two possible relationship scenarios
for this couple type. The first type of couple has accepted
the current status of their sexual connection and are both
okay with a loving relationship without sex—or they
have gone the route of some sort of open relationship.
These couples rarely continue the sexual enhancement
exercises together. The other scenario occurs when one
partner, often in mid-life, has a new dissatisfaction with
the lack of sex or sexual intensity. Before considering
opening or ending the relationship, he wants to explore
what can be salvaged of their sexual connection and
wants to try these exercises. The prognosis often depends
upon how long they have been sexually disconnected, but
regaining desire in both partners is often a difficult—if not
impossible—task. I would suggest this couple see if they
have a different experience by repeating Exercise One.
Subsequent exercises may prove futile for Couple Type
#5, but I encourage couples to go as far in the process as

they feel comfortable. It will surely open dialogue and help the couple better prepare to make decisions about where they go from here as presented in the next chapter and next section of this book. The dialogue helps the couple share their honest feelings, and the discussion itself brings greater closeness and respect.

Couple Type #6

This couple found much sadness, confusion and/or emotional turmoil as they attempted to work the exercise. One partner was overwhelmed with feelings related to control or being controlled—a problem often traceable to early childhood abuse and/or trauma. The affected partner and the couple, in this situation, would be directed to seek professional help as soon as possible. *I strongly advise against continued self-directed sensate focus work in cases where past traumas have not been addressed.*

Once you have a sense of which couple type you and your partner most closely resemble, follow the associated recommendation for repeating Exercise One, going on to Exercise Two, or terminating sensate focus work.

> *I strongly advise against continued self-directed sensate focus work in cases where past traumas have not been addressed.*

Exercise Two: Touch and Vulnerability

There are two parts to this exercise for each partner, and you are encouraged to complete the entire experience in one session. You need to reserve about ninety minutes for the entire exercise.

The purposes of the exercise are to continue to explore non-genital touch, to continue to develop verbal and nonverbal communication strategies for your needs and desires, and to continue to build intimacy through increasing vulnerability. As self-acceptance and positive body image are important for sensual and sexual pleasure, this exercise also provides an opportunity to focus on those aspects of your body that you like and enjoy and to share those with your partner. Create a supportive environment and follow the same *Ten Important Guidelines* you did in Exercise One on page 97. The partner who was in the role of giver first in Exercise One will also be giver first in this exercise.

Part 1: Touch

You are to follow the same instructions you did in Exercise One, except this time the *receiver* is in control. The receiver will take the hand of the giver and place it, in a loving manner, wherever he wants on his body. Again, the receiver will *exclude* nipples, buttocks, perineum and genitals. The receiver, taking full responsibility for his own comfort and interests moves the giver's hand, directs the amount of speed and/or pressure, and/or verbally instructs his partner on where and how to touch. The receiver may ask for lotions, oils or powders, and the receiver makes the choices for creating a romantic setting (i.e., flowers, candles, etc.), but the lights are to remain on, as always, for the exercise.

It is the intention of the receiver to develop loving communication strategies—both verbal and nonverbal—for directing his partner's touch. The receiver is taking responsibility for his own interests throughout the experience by asking for what he wants. The giver wants to learn and appreciate what interests his partner. Keeping the exercise to about fifteen minutes face down, and then fifteen minutes face up, the receiver should be the one to announce when the time limit is reached.

Once the time limit is reached, you will want to change giver and receiver roles and repeat part one.

When you have each completed both roles in Part One, go immediately into Part Two of this exercise.

Part 2: Vulnerability

The man who started as receiver in Part One will go into Part Two by standing naked in front of a full-length mirror. His partner will sit naked nearby looking into the mirror at his partner. Both partners are to observe the *reflection* of the body of the man standing *without judgment*. Do *not*, at any point, turn to face one another directly. Taking your time to simply observe, after several minutes the man standing is to describe for his partner those parts of his body he likes, enjoys and/or finds attractive. Do *not* point out or focus on anything about your body you do not like. Observe the curves and lines of the body and note how they change with different poses. Bending, flexing a muscle, twisting or squatting may enhance a feature. Changing your facial expression, smiling or tilting your head may create an endearing appearance. Be creative, move your body and have some fun. Be sure your self-description includes gratitude for the way your body looks, feels and moves. Go head to toe.

For this part of the exercise you may touch anywhere on *your own* body. As such, don't forget to observe your genitals. Lift your penis and look at your scrotum and perineum. If you have foreskin, pull it back and forward. Hold your genitalia and move your pelvis to accentuate your "jewels." Have fun observing, with your partner, the wonder of your own body.

Now the killer: spend a full *ten minutes* on Part Two of this exercise with each partner. Use a clock or timer that is not visible to the partner standing. Don't worry about the time and don't skimp on the time. You are creative enough to enjoy the splendor of your body for a full ten minutes! When the ten minutes are completed, the sitting partner announces "time's up," and you may reverse roles.

When both partners have had their turns, take a few minutes to lie together in silence. Give some thought to what it was like to have this experience with your partner. Upon completion, make your date to dialogue, and review the following Questions to Ponder in preparation for your dialogue.

Questions to Ponder:

1. In Part One of this exercise, were there any surprises? Did you learn anything new about yourself or your partner? How did it feel as giver to have your touch directed by your partner? Was there any difference in how it felt to be giver or receiver compared to the same role in Exercise One? Discuss your feelings, your preferences and any new discoveries with your partner.

2. In Part One, were you ever out-of-the moment, anxious, bored or uncomfortable? If so, share possible reasons and/or concerns with your partner.

3. In Part One, if there was sexual arousal, discuss with your partner your feelings about it or any discrepancy in arousal (i.e., one partner was aroused and one not).

4. Did you ever close your eyes and fantasize? How might you share this fantasy with your partner? Share with your partner any and all pleasurable or joyous moments you experienced in Part One.

5. For Part Two of this exercise, what was it like to stand naked and describe your body in front of your partner? Were you able to stay away from any negative judgment of your body? Discuss with your partner any discomfort or feelings of vulnerability.

6. As you observed your partner's body, were there parts of his body that you suddenly found different or more attractive than you remember? Were you aroused sexually by your partner's body or movements? Be sure to share this with your partner.

7. Were you able to have fun with Part Two? Share any moments of joy with your partner.

8. Many men find the mirror exercise creates intense vulnerability, leading to a new closeness with their partner. Was such a shift apparent to you? Discuss the impact of this experience with your partner.

9. Did you become more aware of any physical attributes of your partner that you once found erotically desirable but no longer do? Does it impact your sexual connection? How might you address this with your partner?

Follow the same guidelines for your date to dialogue as you did with Exercise One. At some point soon after your talk with your partner, go back and answer for yourself the same *Questions to Ponder After Exercise Dialogues* you reviewed after Exercise One on page 100.

Before going on to Exercise Three, be sure you feel complete with your partner about Exercise Two. The mirror exercise is tough for some men. If you or your partner found it difficult to keep the focus on the positive aspects of your body, try repeating Part Two at some point in the near future. Learning to accept, love, enjoy and respect your body and its movement are important to being physical with your partner.

And, as with Exercise One, if any disturbing thoughts or past traumatic experiences arise, do not continue these exercises. Instead, seek professional assistance.

Exercise Three:
Sensual Responsiveness

Begin by creating the supportive environment and, as you have in the first two exercises, follow the *Ten Important Guidelines* on page 97.

The purpose of this exercise is to take your partner on a tour of the sensual responsiveness of your erogenous zones. Having completed the first two exercises, you now know what your partner likes to have touched and how he likes to be touched. You have some new verbal and non-verbal communication strategies. For this experience, you are still going to focus on sensation and *not* sex or orgasm, and you are going to continue to take responsibility for *your own* comfort and pleasure.

If you were giver first in the last exercise you will be receiver first this time. The first twenty minutes (ten minutes face up, ten minutes face down) you will touch as you have in the previous exercises, avoiding genitals, nipples, buttocks and perineum. The receiver may use verbal and nonverbal communication to request the desired touch. The receiver may also decide upon the sparing use of any lotions, oils or powders.

In the second twenty minutes or so the giver may touch nipples, buttocks, perineum and genitals. The receiver will completely direct the giver by keeping his hand on top of the giver's hand so the receiver gets what he wants. Take the giver on a sensual tour of your nipples, buttocks, perineum and genitals. If there is arousal, that is fine. If not, that is fine.

There is to be no kissing or use of the tongue, no penetration of the mouth or anus with fingers, tongue or penis, and no stroking of the penis that could stimulate orgasm. This exercise is only about feeling pleasure and giving pleasure.

Once both partners have been giver and receiver, spend some silent time in bed together. You may wish to touch and hold one another, but keep the physical connection *sensual*, not sexual. Complete this exercise by setting a date to dialogue. Review the following Questions to Ponder before your talk.

Questions to Ponder:

1. Did you learn anything new about your own or your partner's erogenous areas? Discuss any new points of pleasure with your partner.

2. How did you feel, as receiver, being able to direct your partner? How did this feel as giver? Discuss with you partner how giving direction may play out in your sexual life together.

3. Was there any sexual arousal for you or your partner? If so, how did it feel to be touched genitally without taking it to orgasm? If there was no arousal, was that disappointing? Discuss any and all feelings about arousal in this exercise recalling that arousal is not important in achieving the purpose of the exercise.

4. Did you go further than the exercise intended? If you or your partner did come close to, or experience, orgasm, consider repeating the exercise without allowing climax.

5. Did you ever close your eyes and fantasize? Share your fantasies with you partner and how they played into any feelings of sexual arousal. If sexual template challenges are an issue, discuss your feelings and concerns.

Follow the same guidelines for your dialogue as in the past, and review the *Questions to Ponder After Exercise Dialogues* on page 100.

If you did experience arousal with genital touch in Exercise Three, you may be asking yourself how you can stay with the *sensual* and not the sexual. The question of "when sex begins" becomes an issue. Remembering that the sexual response cycle actually starts with desire, we can learn how taking time for sensual connection may raise feelings of sexual desire. There are sexologists in the field who argue that _seduction_ is actually the first step in the response cycle, and couples in long-term relationships forget to court their partners in order to create desire. Creating a supportive environment and setting a romantic atmosphere are important components of seduction. (There will be more to learn about seduction and fantasy in Chapter Six.)

When you feel complete with Exercise Three it is time to move to Exercise Four. As we move into Exercise Four and more _sexual_ touch, be aware of the importance of seducing your partner verbally and nonverbally and creating a supportive, romantic and seductive environment. Clear your mind of expectations and know that whatever unfolds will be just fine and a part of the growth process with your partner.

... **seduction** is actually the first step in the response cycle, and couples in long-term relationships forget to court their partners in order to create desire.

Exercise Four: Oral Play and Self-Sex

You are about to start another two-part exploration, the purpose of which is to add an oral and playful dimension to the sensual experience and to observe your partner making love to himself. As we begin to move from a more sensual experience to a more sexual exploration, the guidelines will need to shift a bit. You will create a supportive environment but rather than follow the _Ten Important Guidelines_ as you have in past exercises, you will follow these _Seven Key Guideposts_:

1. Do everything slowly, so that you have time to feel both physically and emotionally.

2. All feelings are okay, even sadness, boredom or anger—should they arise. Allow yourself the full range of emotional experience.

3. Have _no_ expectations. Stay in the moment with your partner.

4. If you get aroused sexually—or don't get aroused—it makes no difference.

5. Take care of yourself. Focus on your own sense of well-being and the sensations that arise. Take responsibility for your own comfort. Let go of everything that is not about the touch you are experiencing, both as giver and receiver.

6. Do *not* use alcohol or drugs before, during or immediately after the exercise.

7. Climax to ejaculation only as specifically directed in the exercise.

Part 1: Oral Play

Flip a coin to decide who will be giver and who will be receiver first. Start with ten or fifteen minutes of touch with the focus on sensation as you have done in the past—avoiding the genitals, buttocks, nipples and perineum. Once relaxed, begin to enjoy extending pleasure into those highly sensuous areas. Enjoy touch anywhere and everywhere as directed by the *receiver* verbally and nonverbally.

At any time you may now feel free to kiss sweetly or deeply. Ask the receiver how he likes to be kissed. Many partners are afraid to teach their lovers new ways to kiss for maximum pleasure. Now is the time to demonstrate, try something new and take your kissing to a new level. Relax the muscles of your face and attempt to kiss without making kissing sounds. Enjoy each other's lips and tongue in a slow, relaxed manner. Don't poke with the tongue. Try licking or gently biting your partner's lips and tongue. As giver, have fun with your tongue as the receiver now directs you to explore his entire body with his tongue. As the receiver, talk about where and how you want to be tongued. You may direct your partner to go head to toe, including the erogenous zones you discovered to be particularly exciting in Exercise Three. The giver may be directed to go down on his partner, and the receiver may be descriptive—or even graphic—with his directions. (For example, "Start by licking my balls and work your way up my cock. Then suck on the head of my dick until I tell you to stop.")

Combine touch with the hands along with your oral exploration. The giver should be focused on pleasing his partner *and* enjoying his own experience. The giver may refuse if it is uncomfortable to follow through on any particular request.

Play for about thirty minutes before attempting Part Two. *At no time* in Part One of this exercise are you to come close to ejaculation.

Fellatio

Paul Joannides, in his book *Guide to Getting It On,* gives some guidelines and information on fellatio (technically, oral stimulation of the penis, but commonly thought of as simply "oral sex") that may be helpful as you introduce an oral dimension to the exercises.

A dry mouth is not conducive to oral stimulations. Start by being sure your mouth, tongue and lips are moist. The more saliva generated, the better, and—because putting anything in the mouth increases salivary flow—just getting started will increase mouth moisture. However, if you are exceedingly dry, begin by drinking some water and/or sucking on a lozenge for a while.

Don't feel that you need to start by taking your partner's entire penis in your mouth. Use your tongue to lick, kiss and flick the shaft of his penis. Run your lips up and down the sides of his shaft and enjoy taking the scrotum—and even the testicles—between your lips to play.

114

When going down on your partner, remember that the top of the penis is the most sensitive. Take him in your mouth as far as is comfortable for both of you. Communicate about gagging if it becomes an issue. The receiver also needs to communicate if there is discomfort, from his partner's teeth for example.

Once you have sufficient salivary lubrication, take your partner in your mouth and create a seal with your lips. Just riding the shaft up and down with this seal should create adequate suction to highly stimulate your partner. However, you may wish to enhance this vacuum by additionally sucking inward. If you and your partner are comfortable riding the entire shaft of the penis, that is fine.

A combination of hand and oral stimulation is often the most satisfying for the person receiving.

You may also choose to use your hand at the base of the shaft and continue with oral stimulation at the top of the penis. *A combination of hand and oral stimulation is often the most satisfying for the person receiving.* Be sure to keep the entire penis lubricated with saliva.

Twisting your head from side to side as you go up and down—as well as using your tongue to stimulate the underside of the penis—can increase sensation. If your partner is uncircumcised, you may wish to use your tongue to explore between the shaft and foreskin or pull the foreskin gently back with each outstroke. Maximum stimulation may be achieved by holding the foreskin back with one hand as you orally stimulate the very sensitive head of the uncovered penis.

At any time, if you are getting tired, take a break from sucking to caress, kiss and lick your partner's penis. Use your hand and saliva to keep your partner stimulated until you are ready to take him in your mouth again.

As you are performing fellatio, use your other hand to caress or massage the inner thighs, play with his nipples, finger the perineum, fondle the scrotum or tease the anal opening. *Most importantly, take your time and mentally focus on the beauty of your partner's penis and how much enjoyment you both receive by sharing it with one another.* The more you get into the excitement of the flesh, the more saliva you will generate, the more intense the fellatio will become, and the more pleasure you and your partner and you will receive.

A note about so-called "deep-throating" or taking the penis beyond the constriction of your throat: most people are unable to accomplish this feat without gagging and/or discomfort. Deep-throating should *not* be a goal and is certainly not necessary for total enjoyment of oral stimulation. If you are very comfortable as a couple with oral sex, you can try to take your partner's penis in this manner. Stimulating the penis with the constriction of the throat can be a highly charged and exciting form of oral sex, but tends to be so only for a small number of "talented" men.

Most importantly, take your time and mentally focus on the beauty of your partner's penis and how much enjoyment you both receive by sharing it with one another.

Part 2: Self-Sex

Go immediately into Part Two with the same receiver and giver roles.

The receiver is now going to make love to *himself* as his partner watches without touching. Be loving to yourself. Touch to please yourself anywhere and *everywhere* you wish.

Close your eyes and fantasize if you like.

Enjoy a minimum of fifteen minutes before reaching orgasm. You may ejaculate if you wish, but if you cannot—or choose not to—that is fine.

Whether you did or did not ejaculate, ask you partner to hold you, caress you or stroke you as you desire. If you did experience climax, you will find yourself in the resolution (refractory) phase of the sexual response cycle. The refractory phase is characterized by a need to relax, rest and recover. Having your head, neck or shoulders rubbed can be extremely calming, reassuring and connecting. Lie together, or ask for whatever you need to feel safe and loved. The receiver should be the one to decide when the exercise is complete.

It is recommended you wait a minimum of two hours before reversing roles and repeating the exercise, beginning again with Part One. Most men prefer to do reverse roles on a different day.

Once both partners have had the chance to give and receive, set a date to dialogue as you have in the past, and review the following Questions to Ponder before your discussion.

Questions to Ponder:

1. Did you learn anything new about yourself or your partner? Did you learn anything new about kissing, fellatio or oral stimulation? Share with you partner any new discoveries and how you might incorporate them into your sexual repertoire.

2. Did you ever feel uncomfortable or challenged by the exercise? What were the feelings? Share these challenges with your partner and see if you can find ways to work around those in the future.

3. Were you able to be aroused? How about your partner? Was there a difference in levels of arousal? Talk with your partner about the fact that arousal is nice but not necessary for physical connection and intimacy. (If E.D. is a problem, discuss possible solutions as presented in Chapter Four.)

4. Were any sexual template challenges magnified by this exercise? If so, consider how this happened, and discuss them with your partner.

5. Did you close your eyes in either part of the exercise? Were you in fantasy? Talk with your partner about your fantasies and share how it feels to know your partner may be fantasizing about someone or something else. We will discuss fantasy more in Chapter Six, but for now know that it is okay to use your imagination at any time in these exercises.

6. What was it like to masturbate in front of your partner? What was it like to watch your partner masturbate? If in the future one of you feels like having sex and the other does not, could you ask your partner to just watch you masturbate? Discuss these feelings with one another.

7. Were you able to ejaculate? If not, how did it feel to have this experience without climax? Recall that orgasm does not matter here as the intimacy of your physical connection is not about arousal or climax but is about sharing the feelings of the exploration with your partner.

8. What was it like to engage in the refractory period with one another? Did you feel safe and connected? Explore your feelings with one another about the afterglow. In retrospect, is there anything additional you would have liked your partner to do for you?

9. Do you feel closer to your partner after this exercise? Talk to each other about the feelings you are experiencing as you take this journey together.

As with the earlier exercises, review the _Questions to Ponder After Exercise Dialogues_ on page 100.

Most men who arrive at this point feel positive about the experience. If you have made it this far you are likely finding yourself feeling closer and closer to your partner emotionally, even if not physically. Only repeat Exercise

Four if you sense you missed or glossed over some aspect of it, leaving you without closure.

Of course, it is also great to just repeat Part Two of the exercise at any time if you want to get off and your partner is not in the mood. For couples with a discrepancy in desire, watching a partner masturbate can be a truly satisfying and connecting experience. It relieves any sort of pressure on the observing partner if he is only asked to watch. It is still an intimate activity, and being watched can be a real turn on for many men. It is perfectly okay to masturbate in front of your partner while he watches. It can be such a freeing experience that the observing partner may become aroused just watching, thereby triggering mutual sexual activity.

Exercise Five: Stimulation to Orgasm

The purpose of this exercise is to begin to involve your partner in your stimulation to orgasm. If you were giver first in Exercise Four, you will be receiver first for this exercise.

Create the supportive environment, follow the *Seven Key Guideposts* on page 112, and then simply repeat Part One of Exercise Four.

Then, instead of going into self-pleasure to reach ejaculation, allow your partner to take you to orgasm orally or manually—or both.

The receiving partner should not self-stimulate unless he is unable to climax to orgasm after *twenty minutes* of stimulation by his partner. At that point, if the receiver still wishes to ejaculate, he may masturbate to orgasm. Remember, maintaining an erection or achieving orgasm is *not* necessary, or even important, for completion of this exercise.

The exercise is complete when the *receiver* decides it is over, and, as with Exercise Four, you will want to spend time in mutual touch and holding through the refractory phase.

As with Exercise Four, it is recommended you wait a minimum of two hours before reversing roles or you can repeat the exercise in reverse on another day. When both partners have had the chance to give and receive, as you have in the past, set a date to dialogue and review the following Questions to Ponder before your discussion.

Questions to Ponder:

1. Did you learn anything new about yourself or your partner in Exercise Five? Share any new discoveries with your partner.

2. Did this exercise ever leave you feeling uncomfortable or challenged? Share your feelings with your partner.

3. Were you able to be aroused? How about your partner? Was there a disturbing difference in levels of arousal? If so, discuss it with your partner. Also discuss any sexual template issues that may be involved.

4. Did you close your eyes during the exercise? Share any fantasies with your partner.

5. Were you able to ejaculate either with or without your partner's help? If not, do you have a sense of why it was difficult, and would you like to try this exercise again? Remember, it does not matter if there was arousal or climax, it is just important to share the feelings with your partner.

6. How did it feel both as giver and receiver to (attempt to) bring each other to climax? Share your feelings—including any pleasure, frustration, anxiety, etc.

7. What was the refractory connection like this time? Did you ask for something you wanted that you did not receive in the previous exercise? Explore your feelings about the afterglow with your partner.

Upon completion of your dialogue, as before, review the *Questions to Ponder After Exercise Dialogues* on page 100.

Having completed Exercise Five, you must be commended for pushing through some difficult discussions and creating vulnerability with your partner.

For many men, at this point, the exercises are feeling too scripted to continue. Others are burning out. Others may feel they have gone as far as they need to for reestablishing a physical and intimate connection. The final two exercises begin to involve anal penetration as an option, and for couples who are not so inclined, Exercise Five may be the end of the line. I encourage even those couples who are not into anal sex to go as far as they can with Exercise Six. You may be surprised to learn more about yourself and your partner by forging ahead.

Exercise Six: Explore Anal Stimulation

The purpose of this exercise is to explore the sensations of anal stimulation and pleasure experienced by you and your partner as you take your positions of choice as a top or a bottom. While anal penetration is encouraged in this exercise, if you are not at all into anal exploration, that is fine, as oral penetration can substitute. In fact, in either case, you will start with oral play, and it will be your choice in the moment as to whether or not to proceed with anal penetration.

I encourage the use of condoms for all anal penetration as discussed in Chapter One for safe sex practices, and recommend that you prepare for that before beginning.

If you do intend to do the anal penetration portion of this exercise, be sure your fingernails are trimmed and smooth to prevent discomfort and/or tearing of anal tissues. Most anal play occurs in the anal canal, which is typically free of fecal material. Penetration may include the lower rectum, however, and there may be some material in this portion of the bowel. Penetration in the presence of fecal matter may increase the urge to defecate, making anal play less than comfortable for the receiver. As well, for some couples, the presence of feces is a turn off. Anal douching is a simple solution to these problems.

An optional precursor to Exercise Six is to have the receiver clear the anal canal and lower bowel prior to play. The easiest and most convenient method is to use a store-bought enema (such as the "Fleet" brand). Empty its contents as the chemical solutions in these enemas are harsh and unnecessary for our purposes. Refill the bottle with warm water, and lubricate both the tip and the anus with a latex-compatible lubricant to prevent condom damage later. Insert the tip as far as you are comfortably able into the anal canal and empty the water into your bowel. Sit down on the commode, and when the urge to defecate is strong *gently* release the contents. Take your time emptying your bowel, being sure not to use force or strain. Repeat the process until the water runs free of fecal material. You may also purchase enema syringe bowls or bags or a shower hook-up for the same purpose.

You are now ready to begin Exercise Six. Create a supportive environment as you have in the past and follow the *Seven Key Guideposts* on page 112.

> *I encourage the use of condoms for all anal penetration...*

When you are ready, start by getting undressed and spending a few minutes just holding, hugging and caressing your partner while standing. Use touch gently to seduce your partner into the shower. Take a nice relaxing warm shower together, soaping each other up, holding each other, kissing and taking turns feeling the soapy lather on each other's body. Wash each other's genitals, buttocks and anal openings. If you are both comfortable with it, you may gently insert a soapy (lubricated) finger into the anus of your partner. Rinse off, dry each other off, and take one another to bed, where the inviting environment should already be set and ready to begin.

The man who is usually the bottom in your relationship will be receiver first. If there are no defined roles, if both of you are bottoms, if both of you are versatile, or if both of you are tops, flip a coin to determine who will be receiver first.

The receiver begins by directing his partner to touch him wherever and however the giver chooses. Start with non-genital touch for ten minutes or so before moving to erogenous areas. Add kissing and use your tongue. Be playful for another ten to twenty minutes. Once stimulated and ready, the receiver should direct the giver to perform oral sex on him. The receiver will want to be sure to be specific as to what feels good and what does not. If you are not aroused, that is fine. Simply direct your partner to use his tongue or hands on your body in a pleasing manner. Continue for another five to ten minutes.

If the receiver is aroused and doesn't wish to be penetrated, he may have his partner take him to orgasm with his hand, mouth or both.

In the refractory phase, the receiver may ask to be held or stroked by his partner. Wait at least two hours before changing roles.

If the receiver is aroused and *does* wish to explore anal pleasure, it is important that the giver assure the receiver that if anything is uncomfortable at any time he will stop and proceed only at the receiver's request. Once this understanding is *verbally* affirmed, the giver should lubricate the receiver's anal opening, as well as his own middle finger, with a latex-compatible lubricant.

While the receiver lies on his back with his knees up and legs spread, the giver should take a comfortable position between his partner's legs. At this point, eye-to-eye, you both are to take some nice deep breaths. The receiver will notice that exhaling is the perfect opportunity to allow the anal sphincter muscle to relax. The giver can explore and massage the anal opening. After several minutes, slowly and gently slide the lubricated finger into the anus. Both partners will notice how the sphincter muscle tightens on inhalation and relaxes on exhalation.

As the relaxation deepens with the receiver's attention to his breath, the giver may begin to enter and observe his partner's reaction. If there is resistance, the giver should back out and continue to massage the anal opening. If there is pleasure, he should continue to enter and explore. The giver may use his other hand to rub his partner's leg, inner thigh, lower abdomen or perineum.

The giver should then make the finger penetrations deeper, and explore the walls of the anal canal without poking, always being gentle and continuously taking note of his partner's reactions to the exploration. The receiver may wish to tighten and loosen the sphincter, taking note of how it feels to do so, as well.

The anus is highly erotic and sensuous because of the thousands of nerve endings in the area. Additionally, for many men, massaging the prostate can stimulate orgasmic contractions and intense pleasure. Once both parties are comfortable with finger play, the giver may begin prostate massage. The prostate is located about three inches into the canal, on the abdominal ("front") side of the canal. The giver, keeping his hand palm up, should curl his finger forward (toward the receiver's belly) to begin massage. During early stages of excitement the prostate will feel soft. As it is massaged, it will become engorged with blood and will feel more firm. Notice that it is about an inch in diameter and oval in shape. The giver must be gentle in rubbing the full extent of the prostate, as poking the prostate would not be fun for the receiver. The giver needs to remain vigilant of any discomfort for his receiver, as well as noting any sensations of pleasure and enjoyment as a precursor to anal penetration.

For receivers who now wish to be anally penetrated by their partner's penis, the *giver* is to lie on his back and the receiver is to mount his partner. You will be invited to explore other positions in Exercise Seven, but, for now, *the bottom is on top and the top is on the bottom.* Additional use of lubricant and a condom are necessary for safety.

To start, the *receiver* will do all of the moving. The giver will not thrust. Take your time. If the giver loses his erection, that is fine. Go back to oral or manual play, or sensate focus, and try again later. The object is for the receiver to enjoy being penetrated, letting his partner know what speed of movement, direction (angle) of penetration and length of stroke he finds most pleasurable.

> ❧
>
> *Direction of penetration is critical to the bottom's comfort, as well as the top's ability to penetrate deeply.*
>
> ❧

Direction of penetration is critical to the bottom's comfort, as well as the top's ability to penetrate deeply. The rectum is not a straight tube and, as such, the angle of insertion needs to conform to the shape of the anal canal in order to minimize discomfort and maximize pleasure. The anal canal bends first toward the front of the body and then takes a turn to the back of the body (see Appendix Four). If the penis is directed at an angle more to the bottom's front side it may hit up against the rectal wall, poking the prostate and causing discomfort. Be sure to angle the penis toward the bottom's back to minimize this discomfort. It is recommended, for this exercise, that the bottom be on top so he might better control the angle of insertion, the depth of penetration and the speed for his comfort.

The receiver may masturbate, or may ask his partner to manually please him. The receiver may also wish to try squeezing the sphincter or push out to explore this feeling for himself and observe how this is for his partner. At the receiver's direction, the giver may thrust—taking care not to cause displeasure and taking note of the angle of penetration. It is perfectly fine if either partner loses his erection. If either partner wishes to stop that is to be respected.

At any time after the receiver gives the okay, either or both partners may climax. Removing the penis after ejaculation must be slow and deliberate both for the comfort of the receiver and to be sure there is no spillage or breakage of the condom. If the position did not lend itself to ejaculation, that is okay. If one or both partners did not climax but wish to, repeat part two of Exercise Four separately, sequentially or simultaneously watching masturbation to ejaculation.

Once complete, enjoy the afterglow together as you have in the past.

If you wish to reverse roles, repeat the exercise on a different day. Thereafter, set a date to dialogue and review the Questions to Ponder prior to your talk.

(Much of the experience in this exercise is based on Jack Morin's book *Anal Pleasure and Health*, and you may wish to read his work for more comprehensive information.)

Questions to Ponder:

1. Did you learn anything new about yourself or your partner in Exercise Six? Were there any surprises? What did you learn about anal penetration? Discuss the experience with your partner.

2. How was the shower and seduction time with your partner? Talk with your partner about the importance to you of building sexual tension before going to bed.

3. If you were the receiver (bottom), was it helpful to be on top? Did you feel in control? If you were the giver (top), how did it feel to be on the bottom? Did you feel a lack of control? Did the position help to explore insertion angle, depth of penetration and/or speed? Discuss with your partner matters of control, as well as any new understandings of penetration as a couple.

4. Was maintaining an erection or ejaculating difficult? If yes, share with your partner your feelings and what might be helpful in the future.

5. Did you reverse roles? Was this out of the norm for you as a couple? Discuss any challenges, feelings and whether you think you might want to try role reversal again.

6. Do you feel you and your partner are sexually compatible in terms of position preference? If not, explore any feelings you have honestly and fully with your partner. What does it mean for your sexual relationship?

7. How was your afterglow time with your partner? Discuss any thoughts or feelings that came up as you lay in bed together.

8. In preparation for Exercise Seven, begin to talk with your partner about other positions that are possible for anal penetration. Do you have some favorites or some you do not like? Discuss the ups and downs of positioning with your partner.

As in the past, review the _Questions to Ponder After Exercise Dialogues_ on page 100. Realize that many couples who have been together for years with waning physical intimacy simply do not have the sexual passion necessary to succeed at anal penetration. Making the attempt is commendable, but can bring up some frustrations and feelings of loss. Be sure you talk through these feelings with your partner. If they are intense, psychotherapy can be an essential resource.

Exercise Seven: Positions for Pleasure

The purpose of Exercise Seven is to negotiate positions for pleasure and discover what it is like to give and receive simultaneously. You have already begun preparation for this exercise by discussing positions for penetration.

Spend a moment or two deciding which positions you might be willing to try for your partner's pleasure in this exercise. For example, top on his back, bottom on his back with his legs up, bottom on his tummy with his legs spread, bottom on his knees with his butt up, leaning over the bed (or chair or table), etc. You also want to discuss who will be the top and who will be the bottom for this exercise. If there is a standard in your relationship, start with that and, if you desire, you can reverse roles and repeat the exercise. If there is no standard for your relationship, flip a coin to choose who will be top and bottom first, and reverse roles for a second time through. If you do reverse roles, repeat the exercise on a different day.

As always, create a supportive environment and follow the *Seven Key Guideposts* on page 112 for this exercise.

Start by having the bottom give and the top receive non-genital touch for ten to fifteen minutes. Switch roles and repeat.

Once you have both enjoyed non-genital sensate focus, move slowly but deliberately into genital touch without concern for who is the giver and who is the receiver. Be playful. Add kissing and oral stimulation. Do what you know to please yourself and your partner. Simply let go and enjoy one another. Notice how it feels to now focus on giving and receiving pleasure simultaneously. Try a "69" position for oral sex. If you'd like, alternate giving and receiving spontaneously, or communicate about it as you play. Ask for what you want, share and be open. Continue for 20 to 30 minutes.

For couples who do not wish to attempt penetration, feel free to ejaculate—individually, simultaneously, sequentially, orally or manually. If there is no orgasm for one or both partners, that is fine.

Remember to hold and support one another with love in the refractory phase.

For those couples who wish to experience anal pleasure and penetration, you may repeat the warm shower, anal douche, and finger penetration as you did in Exercise Six.

Use safer sex practices and try the positions you discussed earlier. Remember to breathe and to be aware and experiment with angle of entry for maximum comfort and pleasure. Talk about how the positions feel as you explore. Notice which ones allow you to focus on your own pleasure and which ones allow you to focus on giving pleasure. See if you are able to find a position or two that maximize(s) simultaneous pleasure for both of you.

Feel free to ejaculate during penetration in any position, or orally or manually. If there is no orgasm, that is fine.

Remember to hold and support one another with love in the afterglow.

When you are complete, set a date to dialogue and review the following Questions to Ponder.

Questions to Ponder:

1. How was the process of discussing and then exploring various positions with your partner? What were your favorite positions? What positions did not work for you as a couple? Discuss any challenges as well as any conclusions you may have come to that could impact the future of your sexual connection.

2. Did you "69"? What was it like for you? Was it truly possible for you to focus on giving and receiving at the same time? Most men find doing so a challenge. The previous exercises were designed to assign roles so you were able to focus on pleasure for yourself and your partner. If you found doing so helpful, discuss how you might, at times, wish to assign roles when you have physical time or sex with your partner.

3. Were you and/or your partner able to climax? If not, discuss your feelings and decide if you wish to repeat the exercise for a different experience.

4. What were the seduction phase, desire phase, arousal phase, orgasm phase and refractory phase of the exercise like for you and your partner? Discuss the phases and the ways you feel that you might enhance each in the future.

Upon completion of this exercise and your dialogue, you will have started on a journey toward more growth and intimacy in your relationship. It took great courage to move through the physical and emotional vulnerability.

To determine your success as a couple, sit down together in a date to dialogue and discuss your answers to these Questions to Ponder.

Questions to Ponder:

1. Do you feel your ability to communicate about sexual and non-sexual matters has improved?

2. Do you feel more able to ask for what you want both in and out of bed?

3. Do you feel more able to share feelings both in and out of bed?

4. Do you feel more intimately connected with your partner?

5. Do you know more about yourself, your partner and your relationship?

If you answered "yes" to any of these questions, your time was well spent. Congratulations on your success!

With these basic understandings of the current potential of your physical connection, let's take a look at enhancing seduction and sex play in your relationship. Chapter Six will focus on the role of fun, frolic and fantasy to help you enjoy your deepening sexual connection without the constraint of exercises, directions and guidelines.

Chapter **Six**

Creative Intimacy:
Fun, Frolic and Fantasy

I recently had a delightful lunch at the home of some friends who wanted to share a new video on Imago Relationship Therapy. This couple has been together for over thirty years, and both are professionals in the fields of social work and human potentiality.

At the conclusion of the very informative and touching film, we got into a discussion about my favorite topic: sex in long-term gay relationships. I do not know, nor do I want to know, whether these guys are still sexual. I do know that they have an exclusive arrangement with one another, and they feel that it is extremely important to the integrity of their relationship. I highly respect their choice of exclusivity.

Talking to them about making sex work over time with the same man, I was told they believe strongly that watching pornography, going on gay sex-oriented Internet sites and masturbation essentially steal the sexual energy that *should* be reserved for our partners. I honor such an arrangement if that works for them, but I have to say that this generalized understanding of "stealing sexual energy" does not hold up well for most gay men. Such *shoulds* put artificial constraints on sexual expression.

Sexual *Shoulds*

In my opinion, the only restraints on sex are that:

1. it be between consenting adults,

2. there is respect for each partner's limits ("no" means "no"), and

3. there be no irreparable bodily or emotional harm.

As such, I suggest that all other limitations on sexual expression are as agreed to by any two engaging and consenting adults. (There will be more on relationship and sexual agreements in Part Three of this book.)

Empowering your sexual relationship requires lifting any preconceived notions about what a sexual relationship *should* look like. Understand that *shoulds* are simply beliefs you've picked up along life's journey. As discussed in Chapter Two, *beliefs are not inherently true.* A belief is just a thought you think over and over. Beliefs that put constraints on sexual expression, for example, are learned. Almost anything learned can also be unlearned.

Many beliefs about sex have religious and/or cultural underpinnings that require difficult introspection to reconcile with the great variation in human sexual expression. Think about how the belief "sex with someone of the same sex is a sin" affects gay sexual expression. That's a belief that's not worth holding on to if you happen to be gay. Hopefully that's a belief, if you once held, you have already unlearned.

In order to widen the sexual experience with your partner you may have to examine your beliefs and choose to eliminate or change those that limit your experiences. Note, however, that this is not the same as engaging in sexual behavior that does not interest you or could cause physical or emotional harm.

For example, perhaps you do not watch pornography because you believe you *should* not fantasize about anyone but your partner. This could limit your fantasy life—an important ingredient for expanding sexual adventure. Perhaps, as do my friends, you feel it takes away sexual energy that *should* be directed toward your partner and will adversely affect your sexual connection. You might want to put away the *shoulds* and see what happens when you introduce adult films. If you can't dismiss the beliefs, you will not be able to enjoy the visuals or allow fantasy to enhance the sex life you have with your partner. You may even feel disgusted and turned off. As such, your belief will be experienced as a personal truth and will be affirmed. *If you believe something strongly enough, you can always find evidence to support it.*

Beliefs shape our experience, just as experiences shape our beliefs. Beliefs about sex shape our sexual experience, just as sexual experiences shape our beliefs about sex. If you give yourself permission to think differently and test your beliefs, you may find an expansive and different sexual experience. Of course, if you've tried before and you're just not into watching pornography, by all means don't bother. You do know watching it will not cause physical harm. However, a belief that unprotected sexual intercourse is unsafe and could cause bodily harm is a belief worth keeping. That's one belief you do not want to test.

The following Questions to Ponder may help you begin the process of giving thought to your belief systems and how they impact your sexual creativity.

Questions to Ponder:

1. Aside from any beliefs about being gay, what beliefs (shoulds) do you have about sex and various sexual activities that prevent a broader sexual experience? Where did they come from? Do you feel you could change and/or modify any of these beliefs should

> *If you believe something strongly enough, you can always find evidence to support it.*

your partner be interested in a new sexual adventure? Discuss any possibilities with your partner.

2. What limits do you and your partner set for your sexual exploration with one another? Would you like to challenge any of those limits? How might you speak with your partner about making changes?

This chapter includes a number of ideas and strategies for expanding your sexual experience, many of which are introduced in Dagmar O'Connor's *How to Make Love to the Same Person for the Rest of Your Life and Still Love It*. Dr. O'Connor was a student of Masters and Johnson, and her work on long-term sexual intimacy has, to this day, had a vibrant impact on the field of sexology. I conferred with her when writing my doctoral dissertation, and have modified her concepts for gay male couples.

Sexual Energy, Fitness and Selfishness

We spoke about the male sex drive in Chapter One, but many men in long-term relationships with waning sexual activity often put away thoughts of sex completely. In order to reengage sexually with your partner you will want to reinvigorate your interest in sex generally. There is an "inertia" about sexual energy, as there is with all energy. Inertia is the concept that a body at rest stays at rest and a body in motion stays in motion. And, where sex is involved, it's time to get moving.

Don't be afraid to think about sex. Don't be afraid to *talk* about sex. It is okay to give your partner a seductive glance. It is okay to be cruised by other men—and to cruise them. In fact, it is okay to *enjoy* cruising other men and to *enjoy* being cruised by other men. Acknowledging sexual attractiveness in yourself and others is not harmful. Discuss such acknowledgment with your partner to make sure that it is not a threat to your relationship. In fact, as a way to get your sexual energy moving, cruising may even have the potential to increase the sexual interest and energy in your own relationship.

We've already spoken at length about the importance of sound mental health to an intimate relationship. Good physical health is also extremely important. Stay in shape, exercise, eat a nutritious diet low in sugar and fat, maintain good hygiene—especially with your teeth and gums—stay away from drugs and limit alcohol. Your physical health and well-being are inexorably linked to your sexual health and well-being. When you feel good about your physical health and appearance, you feel more sexual and are in better shape for sexual activity.

> *...in order to satisfy your partner sexually, you also must be sexually selfish.*

Any discussion of enhancing sexual intimacy necessarily requires a word about selfishness. Intimacy between partners requires each man to have compassion and empathy, and to focus on the other's needs, desires and well-being. However, *in order to satisfy your partner sexually, you also must be sexually selfish.* At first, this idea creates great angst for couples trying hard to please one another and wanting to make a sexual relationship work. The problem is that sex does not work unless *both* partners are satisfied. Working at pleasing a partner sexually often leads to performance anxiety, feelings of inadequacy and erectile failure. Pleasing your partner in a way that pleases *you* ultimately creates a reciprocation of sexual satisfaction.

As you move through this chapter with creative suggestions for fun, frolic and fantasy, be open to dialogue with your partner about the gratification of your own needs and desires. *When you give yourself permission to be selfish about having your own sexual desires fulfilled, you enhance your partner's willingness to do likewise.* When you hit upon various activities that are mutually self-satisfying you will find that the sexual energy flows easily and effortlessly.

It's all about being about staying in the moment with your partner, if you work at trying to figure out how to please your partner and are not being sexually satisfied at the same time, you are very likely to move out of the moment, destroying the intensity of the sexual connection. Sex is not about work, it's about fun. If you need more evidence that sex is a selfish activity, ask yourself why you often don't feel like pleasing your partner sexually as desire wanes in your relationship. *Your* drive to be sexual is a biological phenomenon meant to stimulate the pleasure centers in *your* brain. *The more you and your partner are creative at exploring ways to be mutually self-gratified, the more fulfilling a sexual connection you will enjoy together.*

> *The more you and your partner are creative at exploring ways to be mutually self-gratified, the more fulfilling a sexual connection you will enjoy together.*

Questions to Ponder:

1. What might you do to move the sexual energy in your life? Discuss with your partner any feelings that come up when you consider these activities.

2. What might you do to improve your fitness for sex? What can you and your partner do together to improve your fitness for sex? Discuss these activities with him.

3. What might you suggest to your partner to satisfy your sexual desires that you think he might not enjoy? Have a discussion with your partner about sexual selfishness and see if there are areas where you both can indulge selfish gratification to enhance your sexual connection.

Dating Your Partner

A prime mover of sexual excitement is the *naughtiness* factor. As we get to know our partners there is a tendency to lose the down-and-dirty of our sexual connection. The beauty of slow, lovemaking sex need not be lost to the desire to experience a little nastiness in bed. We will discuss ways of creating and inspiring your own naughtiness, but understand that sameness leads to boredom and a lack of sexual tension. You will want to break your patterns and break your own rules to stimulate sexual excitement. As discussed in Chapter Three, it is the communication about tension in the relationship that provides the safety and trust necessary to move into sexual risk-taking. When you use the skills for healthy dialogue, sexual adventures with your partner can be both exciting and safe.

The two challenges couples face when reigniting sexual fun and frolic are: (1) how to get it started, and (2) who is going to get it started. Initiation probably won't come as naturally as it might have in the beginning of your sexual relationship. One belief I strongly advise abandoning is the notion that spontaneity is necessary, or even important, for good sex. As couples settle in together, priorities and time allotted for working on their relationship tend to shift. Both partners are working, making time for friends and family, and have social activities and life responsibilities. Life gets busy, and sex seems to take a back seat. When you first meet your passionate partner and all you can think about is your wonderful new man, sex happens. After a time you have to *make* sex happen. I like to say, *you have to plan to be spontaneous!*

...you have to plan to be spontaneous!

You've heard therapists and relationship experts say plan a *"date night"* many times before. Well, you're about to hear it again. A date night does not have to include sex, and it does not have to be at night. I prefer to *think of a date as a time of intimate connection.* The date is about spending time alone together without interruption so you are able to share feelings. *The date is unlikely to happen unless you plan it.* I suggest a regular time minimally on a weekly basis to be blocked out on the calendar. This appointed time must be a top priority for both partners. If you usually go out with friends on a Saturday night, for example, either do not make Saturday night date night, or plan never to see

...think of a date as a time of intimate connection.

friends on a Saturday night. Planning for these date nights is not easy, but somehow we make time every day to be at work from nine to five, only taking off when we are sick or have a real emergency. Why can't we do likewise for our relationships? I know many gay men who diligently work out at the gym five days a week for an hour or more, but can't seem to find a couple of hours of uninterrupted time with their partners. You want to think about your partner and the intimate life you share as a top priority in your life in the same way you think about your work—or your workout.

I have found that the couples who are successful at planning dates are firm in principle, but flexible in procedure. In other words, they may, for example, have "Friday night date night." When they both get home on Friday nights, they have a glass of wine on their balcony, go into the bed and have sex or cuddle time, shower, and go to dinner. But, if they have an out-of-town guest in on a Friday, they will reschedule the date to the Thursday night before. They do not skip date night—just as the man who misses a cardio workout on Monday morning may choose to go to the gym Monday night instead. *The date is a commitment* you make to your partner, to yourself and to your relationship. Once agreed upon, follow through—even when one or both of you is/are not in the mood. You will be surprised to find how often the experience is enjoyable and appreciated when you initially "just didn't feel like it."

Your date can be anything you choose to create emotional intimacy. However, when the intention for your dinner date does include physical intimacy, after a full day and a heavy meal with some cocktails or wine, sleep may be more seductive than sex. You know yourself and your partner. Talk about options. The couple I mentioned in the last paragraph have dinner *after* their physical time together. Some men prefer morning sex. Have a Sunday morning date. Get up and have breakfast in bed with the Sunday paper, and fool around before or after. Or, the partner who gets up first can make coffee, go back to play in bed, and then the two can read the paper and do Sunday brunch… by themselves together. Maybe your date is a Saturday afternoon drive or walk on the beach or in the park. Be creative and realistic. Don't choose a time or activity that you know won't actually work or you won't genuinely enjoy—but don't be afraid to try something new that you think could be awesome if you did. The key points are that the time be regular, alone together, uninterrupted and intimate.

So how do you plan to be spontaneous? The answer lies in seduction and salaciousness. It is all about your imagination and creativity. This chapter has some ideas for you, but you want to make date night your own unique adventure. It is all about *ritual plus variety*. You and your partner know what you know you enjoy. Build on the exercises you completed in Chapter Five, and talk about how to incorporate them into new adventures. The exploration is not over. Your appointment date *plus* a general idea of what will happen and how *plus* an openness to try something new and different *equals* an enriched intimate experience for you both as a couple.

Create romance through seduction.

Setting the scene opens the opportunity for intimate connection. *Create romance through seduction.* You know you're having your date, but surprise your partner with something totally unanticipated. Think about all of your senses and how you might stimulate them for your partner. Dress to entice. Bring a small gift that says "I love you." Touch your partner's face. Make direct eye contact. Play "your" song. Put rose petals on the bed or a note under the pillow. Have some fun! Think love!

Questions to Ponder:

1. What patterns, if any, have created boredom in the bedroom for you and your partner? Discuss with your partner how you might break these patterns.

2. What will work for a regular date in terms of your weekly schedule? Work with your partner to find a mutually agreeable timeframe. Can you shut off your phone and focus totally on your partner?

3. Begin to use your imagination and discuss ways to create a date that has both ritual and variety. In what seductive and salacious ways could you arouse your partner's five senses?

Sexual Fantasy

A primary limiting belief you will want to dispel to have an enjoyable sex life is that fantasy is somehow wrong or "a bad thing." Sex does not happen without fantasy. I like to say you have to *be in fantasy* in order to have sex. Fantasy can be actively seeing, feeling, tasting, smelling or hearing your partner, and being turned on by the eroticism generated by his presence. When you are in the moment with your partner, focusing on this fantasy generates the desire for sexual connection. It is not only normal, but it is *human* to have shifting fantasies during sex. Sure, it's great to be in fantasy about our partner, but it is also wonderful to use the gift of your imagination to enhance, augment or alter the fantasy as you are having sex with a partner. *Man was given the ability to use imagination and fantasy to eroticize the sexual experience.* Denying yourself this ability because you feel it takes you away from your partner produces shame and a disconnection from doing what comes naturally. In fact, you can be fairly certain if you are censuring your fantasies you are censuring your sex. *Censored sex is like kissing through a handkerchief.* You are not going to feel much like doing it.

Most men I have met in long-term relationships, who are still sexual, report an active fantasy life. This fantasy life could be shared or private. While having sex with your

> *Man was given the ability to use imagination and fantasy to eroticize the sexual experience.*

partner, it is okay to fantasize about the way your partner used to look when you first met. It is okay to fantasize about the sexy guy you saw at the gym. It is okay to fantasize about bringing a third into your bedroom. It is okay to fantasize about having your partner tie you up and suck you off. Fantasy is often about that which we do not and will not do in reality. That's why it's called "*fantasy.*" Use your imagination; that's what it's for.

Talk with your partner about sharing fantasies when you're having sex. Some couples are not comfortable doing so, but see if you are able to go beyond your comfort zone. *Sexual ecstasy begins at the end of your comfort zone.* Taking risks in a safe emotional space with your partner by moving to the edge of, and beyond, your usual limits creates the naughtiness and sexual tension discussed earlier.

Talk with your partner in advance about how the *scene* might play out. Maybe the top in your relationship is penetrating another man while the bottom watches. Describe this hot guy and everything you do with him as you and your partner enjoy each other sexually. Maybe you and your partner would like to try a bondage scene, but first want to explore it in fantasy. Describe how you want to be tied up and what you want your partner to do as you are helpless to move about.

You may wish to create an erotic story either leading up to or during sex. You could even read an erotic magazine article or book together and then play out a scene from it. Don't be afraid to *talk dirty*. It's okay to tell someone you love, "Fuck me, baby." Talk loudly if you want. *Scream!* Make noise. Make your fantasy come alive. It's all about being creative in the same way a poet writes a poem or an artist paints a painting. Seduction through sharing erotic illusions and visions can stimulate sex play and widen the sexual exploration with your partner. It is important, when bringing fantasy into the sexual relationship with your partner, that you give and receive permission to move forward with the illusion. A unilateral decision on bringing fantasy out into the open with your partner—without discussion—may create discomfort and diminish the feeling of safety.

Questions to Ponder:

1. Do you have any beliefs about fantasy that you may wish to dispel? Share these with your partner.

2. Have you ever fantasized about other men when having sex with your partner? Talk with your partner about the fantasies you have when you're together sexually.

3. What fantasies can you imagine having that might eroticize your time with your partner? Can you share these in dialogue with your partner? Can you share these in bed with your partner as part of a sexual scene?

Pornography and Paint

Many men find the creative process difficult, and for them fantasy is more easily accessed through the visual and auditory world of pornography. As with sex in general, and as discussed earlier, if you have been taught that porn is wrong, you either have to change your belief or decide not to watch it. I do not advocate the use of porn *per se*, but, in my opinion, there is nothing wrong with using it to stimulate sexual interest and activity.

If you and your partner elect to watch porn together during sex, be sure to discuss the types of adult films you each enjoy. This may include whether the films are amateur or professional, what types of men (and/or women) are shown, and what type of sex is depicted. There may be some activities you've never done and would never do but, nevertheless, find erotic. There may be activities you'd like to learn more about and try with your partner. Decide together if you want to watch before, during and/or after

> *Many men find the creative process difficult, and for them fantasy is more easily accessed through the visual and auditory world of pornography.*

144

your sexual time together. Talk about whether you think this could be a regular activity, perhaps for your date night, or if you prefer more limited exposure. See if it might be fun to watch and then duplicate a scene—either with or without the film running.

If you are not much into watching other men having sex, you may wish to create your own porn. Set up a camera on a tripod or use your smart phone to film yourselves having sex. Or, you can film each other in poses, playing with toys (we will discuss these more, later) or masturbating. Play the video back and watch yourselves having sex while having sex. You might also take still photographs of yourselves naked, seductive, and/or sexually engaged and Photoshop them (or not) to enjoy again before or during sex. The act of photographing or filming each other can be highly erotic. You might also hire a professional photographer who has experience with nudity and sex. Have him (or her) take photographs or film you while you play with your partner. Again, the experience itself—as well as the playback—can feel very naughty and be very sexually charged. (If you try a photographer be sure he/she is truly professional and offers or agrees to sign a confidentiality agreement with you.)

As part of—or separate from—the art of film and photography, you may wish to use your body or your partner's body as a canvas for creativity. Certainly you may play with wardrobe and hair, but why not try painting your partner? Buy some paint, and have some fun. You can paint him as a warrior, or just paint a sun around your partner's navel. Get some erasable magic markers and write on your partner. "Put it here" might be erotic. Painting or writing on your partner's penis can be whimsical and fun. Are tattoos in your template, but not on your partner? Get some temporary tattoos and see if you find increased arousal. You might coat your partner in latex body paints. And, of course, there's always chocolate, whipped cream and a cherry on top for edible erotic art.

(Note to the Reader: While the use of pornography for sex play can be rather innocuous, I want to express my intense opposition to the exploitation of children in the production of pornography. Watching child pornography directly contributes to this exploitation, and it is in direct violation of the guideline that sex always be between consenting adults as previously discussed in this chapter. I also feel that pornography depicting adults engaging in unprotected sexual intercourse or violent sex resulting in physical injury sends a message of irresponsibility, potentially violating the other previously set forth guideline that there be no irreparable bodily harm as a result of sexual activity.)

Questions to Ponder:

1. Are you into watching pornography? Talk with your partner about your feelings about watching sex while having sex. How might adult films sexually recharge your physical connection?

2. What do you think about creating your own erotic movie or photo album? Discuss any possibilities with your partner.

3. How might you get artistic using your body, or your partner's body, as canvas? Discuss possible erotic, creative fun.

Hotel Sex

The bed you sleep in every night with your partner becomes a "sacred" space over time. It is often hard to engage in some naughty, hot, new encounters in the same old bed you've been sleeping, reading, eating and watching TV in for years. Some couples find moving to another room in the house, even a different bed in the house, makes a big difference. Most established couples, though, really need to escape to totally different surroundings. Couples frequently report better sex on vacations, and they attribute the improvement to having time to relax and let go. While this is true, to a large degree it is also the seductive quality of a new bed in romantic surroundings that enhances the sexual energy. Because most of us cannot go on vacation on a weekly basis, my recommendation would be to take a trip to a nearby hotel.

If the occasion is special, an anniversary for example, perhaps you will want to plan a getaway. Make a reservation, take a drive, transform your date night into a "date weekend." Create a romantic setting, buy flowers, a bottle of wine, candles. Try sensate focus and see where it might lead. Plan quiet time together without a lot of "busy-ness." Take walks, bike, lie on a beach, go to the park, and talk, talk, talk.

For the not-so-special occasions, make them special with an overnight—or just a few hours—at a local hotel. Expense may be an issue, but sometimes the cheapest, sleaziest, most run-down places offer the naughtiest, most fun experiences. Maybe you want to create a fantasy rendezvous. Plan to be spontaneous. Talk with your partner about what the scene will be like. Maybe you want to meet there as though you were having an illicit affair. Perhaps you might want to create roles to play. Wear some sexy clothes or undergarments to enhance your fun. Maybe one partner plans to arrive to find his mate undressed, in bed and ready for action. And don't forget to bring your camera.

Public Sex

Keeping with the theme of naughtiness and riskiness, public sex—and the risk of getting caught with your pants down—can be a big turn-on for some men. Be forewarned, however, that public sex is a crime, and getting caught not only creates a criminal record but the embarrassment factor can be huge. That being said, maybe you have access to private outdoor areas that could enhance the fantasy of being caught or observed having sex with your partner. Sometimes private beaches or backyards work just fine, without actually being in public.

There are also, of course, open venues for gay men—such as bathhouses and sex clubs. The thought of using these facilities is a real turn-off for a lot of guys with their reputation for drugs and disease. We will address open relationships in the next part of the book, but going to a bathhouse does not necessarily mean having sex with other men. The sexual energy in a men's club can be astronomical. For men who enjoy the whole scene, going there with your partner and having sex in a public space—or even in your own cubical—can be erotic and fun. Clearly, this is not for everyone, but, with limits, it can add a new dimension to your sexual relationship.

For the more tame and conservative, public displays of affection with your clothes on are a wonderful way to demonstrate the love and attraction you have for your partner. And, for that matter, keeping your clothes on while having sex at home or on the road can be great fun as well.

Questions to Ponder:

1. Have you ever noticed a difference in the physical connection with your partner when you are in a different bed or while on vacation? Discuss the notion of hotel sex with your partner. Fantasize out loud together about what such a trip might be like.

2. What sorts of public sex options, if any, might you and your partner enjoy safely? Have you ever discussed going to a sex club or bathhouse with your partner? How would you feel about such an experience? If both you and your partner think you might like the

experience, be sure to sit down and negotiate *exactly* what such an exploration might look like. (In the context of an open relationship, this might be best discussed after reading Part Three of this book.)

3. How do you feel about public displays of affection? Are you and your partner on the same page in this regard? Discuss possibilities with your partner.

Paraphilias

Paraphilias are often defined as "unusual and/or socially unacceptable forms of sexual imagery or behavior." I prefer to understand paraphilic sex as erotic fantasy and/or engagement other than the so-called normophilic activities of vaginal, oral and anal intercourse. It is not unusual for men to be interested in paraphilic activity. Sexual fantasies and activities that are commonly considered socially unacceptable naturally increase the "naughtiness factor," bringing the sexual energy to higher heights. Oftentimes the fear of a partner's reaction to an interest in paraphilic activity results in personal secrecy. Recalling our discussion of the intimacy created when we transcend our fears and talk to our partners about uncomfortable topics, *I encourage men to discuss their fantasies even if they believe they will not be well received.* Talking does not mean doing, and you may be surprised to learn your partner has a curiosity about the same—or related—interests.

I encourage men to discuss their fantasies even if they believe they will not be well received.

It is important to note that some paraphilic behaviors are considered a mental health problem when the behavior involves non-consenting persons and/or causes significant distress or social impairment. When an individual can only be aroused by paraphilic stimulation there may be significant impairment of an ability to create sustainable intimate relationships. In these situations, it is advised that men seek professional assistance. And, as discussed earlier, any form of sexual activity that is coerced or causes irreparable bodily harm is unacceptable. Let's take a look at some of the more common paraphilic activities you may wish to explore with your partner.

A fairly familiar paraphilia is the fetish. The term "fetish" refers to sexual excitement generated by a non-living object. You often hear people speak of a "foot fetish." You can be sexually interested in feet, but that would not be considered a fetish because feet are part of the *living* human body. However, you *could* have a shoe or a boot fetish. Part of dominance-submission sex might include licking or kissing the boots of a "master." Leather attire, undergarments, diapers or the clothes normally worn by the opposite sex are frequently the objects of fetish desire. (As an interesting side note, transvestism is defined as "cross-dressing" in *heterosexual* men and is not commonly a sexually charged fetish for gay men.)

A more prevalent paraphilic scene in the gay world is "BDSM," a complex acronym encompassing bondage and discipline, dominance and submission, sadism and masochism. BDSM can range from very "light play" with handcuffs to severe, painful punishments such as whipping and beating. There are bondage clubs throughout the world where men of like minds can test their limits. These might include relentless caning, flogging, severe "cock and ball torture," and/or caging for long periods of time.

Your personal exploration with BDSM is likely to be "vanilla," a term used to describe more mild sexual activities such as restraints, handcuffs, blindfolds, spanking or nipple clamps. If you are more adventurous, you may wish to experience light flogging or paddling, ball stretching and/or dildo play. If you wish to try even more, you might go for water sports, fisting or electrosex. "Water sports" refers to urinating on your partner or in his mouth. (You may be surprised to learn that, unless there is a urinary tract infection, urine is actually sterile. However, because urine is high in salt content, the receiver may suffer unpleasant gastric aftereffects if the urine is swallowed.) Fisting, fist fucking or handballing are terms that refer to anal penetration with the hand or fist, often including some length of the arm. Electosex involves using devices that deliver electrical stimulation, often directed onto the penis, scrotum, nipples and/or up into the rectum. I am not going to give details about techniques, but all of these activities require instruction and care to maintain adequate levels of safety. I recommend couples not engage in such explorations without learning from experienced, hands-on teachers.

Many major cities have leather or fetish stores or clubs that provide workshops about many paraphilic activities. So-called "Leather Universities" and leather weekend gatherings in various cities throughout the world and throughout the year would probably provide all the instruction you could possibly desire.

If you and your partner do decide to engage in edgy sex, be sure to agree to a "stop word" with your partner to keep things safe, trusting and comfortable. The word "stop" is not the best word to use because often we exclaim "stop!" automatically before we truly want to end an experience. Find a word that is unlikely to come up during sex, and— when the word is given—be sure that the scene comes to an end.

I do suggest a trip to your local leather or fetish shop as an experience for you and your partner. Even if you're not into any of these more non-vanilla activities, you may find some stimulating grist for your sexual mill. The field trip may spur conversation about some toys or paraphernalia you've been curious about trying. Cock rings, ball stretchers, dildos, butt plugs, vacuum pumps, vibrators, flavored lubricants, colored condoms, nipple clamps, leather accessories, sexy clothes, flimsy undergarments, handcuffs, restraints and blindfolds are just some of the safer and sane items you might take a look at trying to arouse the sexual feelings in your relationship. Don't be afraid to ask a salesman questions about how to use items you are curious about. And if you can't figure out what something is for, ask. The people who work in these establishments generally enjoy sex and talking about their merchandise. They are usually very helpful—sometimes too helpful—in assisting shoppers with trying items on for size.

See if you and your partner might want to pick up a few toys to try out on each other at home or on your date night or weekend. And, if actually using any of these items or trying a new activity is exciting but not something you want to do in real life, use fantasy with your partner to role play and pretend. *Imagination is the key to unlocking your inner world and making it come alive in bed with your partner.*

Imagination is the key to unlocking your inner world and making it come alive in bed with your partner.

Questions to Ponder:

1. Are there any paraphilic sexual activities you are curious about? Get up the courage to have a conversation about them with your partner even if you expect disapproval.

2. Do you and your partner ever play with toys? Discuss the possibility of visiting a sex shop. What sorts of paraphernalia might you want to explore with your partner? Discuss the possibility of having your partner watch you as you experiment with a new toy.

3. Are there any paraphilic behaviors that are just too over-the-top for you to want to actually try, but you find erotically charged? Discuss the possibility of using fantasy out loud with your partner to role play and pretend.

Tech and Tantra

Today's technology has given us some additional toys for sexual play. Sex at a distance is sometimes necessary and, sometimes, just plain fun. If you are going to be physically separated from your partner for a while, perhaps you will want to explore phone sex or cybersex with him. Set a date and time to use your phone or web cam to create an erotic long distance connection. If you are on the phone, tell your partner what you want him to do to himself. Tell your partner what you're doing to yourself. Be graphic and specific. Be sure he can hear your sighs, groans and moans. Breathe hard and be sure, if you climax, to have a very verbally explosive orgasm. Use role play and fantasy if you like, and perhaps pretend you are engaged in some paraphilic sex or sex with another man. If using web cams—as you may have tried with filming—become a porn star for your partner. Show your stuff and don't forget the audio portion of your performance. Have fun with one another, laugh, and enjoy. And, even if your partner is not far away, setting a date for "tech sex" can be a fun diversion to expand your sexual repertoire.

Embracing the latest technological advances necessarily demands a look to ancient times for enhancing sexual intimacy, as well. Tantric sex was born in India around 5000 BC as a response to religious teachings requiring abstinence for enlightenment. Focusing on breathing, meditative and relaxation techniques, as well as using the five senses as tools for soulful connection, Tantra is a spiritual practice designed to expand creative intimacy. There are many tantric teachers and schools that provide instruction for individuals and couples to develop a holistic, spiritual approach to sexual adventure. For instance, The Body Electric School out of Oakland, California, grew out of the need to provide safe sexual outlets for men with HIV.

Questions to Ponder:

1. How might you experience tech sex with your partner? Discuss possibilities for role play, fun and fantasy over the phone or computer.

2. Would you consider a spiritual approach to connecting sexually with your partner? Discuss options that might ~~make a spiritual sexual connection for both of you.~~

3. What other sexual explorations came to mind while reading this chapter? Keep your mind open and your imagination going and discuss the totality of possibilities with your partner.

PART THREE

Creative Relationship Re-Contracting

Relationship Paradigms and Contracts: Creative Intimacy and Permission to Choose

I had the good fortune to visit St. Petersburg, Russia, not long after the fall of the Soviet Union. I recall conversations with several Russians about their new-found freedoms. It seemed that one of the biggest challenges people faced was having "too many" choices. During communism, there had been one brand and one choice. With the opening of markets, the Russian people had to think about what they actually wanted.

> **Freedom to choose opens up vast potential for our lives.**

Freedom to choose opens up vast potential for our lives. Choice also involves difficult decisions, with their associated risks and responsibilities. This chapter will ask you to look at the totality of choices for your unique relationship—in the context of honest self- and mutual-reflection—and then come to a place of compromise and agreement.

I want to state, at the outset, that I have *no* personal or professional opinion, agenda or preference for any particular relationship paradigm. I believe strongly that whatever two people decide for their partnership is unique to them and is to be honored and respected. It is not unusual for us to be intolerant or judgmental of others who make different choices than our own. I ask readers to be open-minded. Not all of the relationship models presented are going to be right for you, but that does not make them wrong for another couple who may be reading this same book. The most critical point to all of this is that men be honest with themselves and honest with their partners about what they truly feel and desire for their lives.

Paradigm Choice

A "paradigm" is a philosophical framework, model or pattern. We often hear about a "new paradigm," meaning a new way of looking at a given situation or set of circumstances. The term "relationship paradigm" refers to the framework within which a couple chooses to interact. This necessarily includes an agreement to be—or not to be—sexually exclusive with a partner. The heterosexual model in our culture holds up the monogamous marriage as the ideal model to emulate. Indeed, the model works very well for a sizeable number of couples (both gay and straight) in our society. In fact, nearly fifty percent of married couples remain in their marriages for life. We do not, of course, know what percentage of married couples remain sexually exclusive throughout their married life because of the difficulty of collecting truthful data, but we might assume the percentage is fairly high.

Once again, I wish to make a distinction between "monogamy" and "exclusivity." Monogamy refers to being married to one person (while polygamy refers to being married to more than one person). Exclusivity is herein defined as *sexual fidelity* with one partner. Many married couples choose not to be exclusive—or simply are not faithful. Religious marriage in a Judeo-Christian society carries with it a presumption that the partners commit to being sexually exclusive with one another.

RELATIONSHIP PARADIGMS AND CONTRACTS

Sexual openness in marriage has been in the process of coming out of its own closet since the sexual revolution of the '60s. The advent of predictable birth control, the growth of women in the workplace, and knowledge of—and access to—different lifestyle choices through the media and the Internet have all contributed to a questioning of the traditional "marriage and exclusivity" paradigm.

Most couples, gay or straight, marry to solidify their commitment and love for one another. But a marriage contract is not necessary to affirm love and commitment. It is a choice. Indeed, any arrangement—whether sanctified by the state or not—is the unique choice of two people who want to be together as a couple. In my opinion, it is not up to the state, the culture, the society, the church, a therapist or anyone else to tell a couple what is best for them contractually and/or sexually. All too often, however, couples do not consciously and mutually decide upon a partnership choice. Many partners make assumptions about their relationship dynamic, and the wishy-washy nature of their understanding (or non-understanding) creates misunderstandings and disappointment. If ever there was a time for you to use the communication skills you developed in Chapter Three, it is when you are in dialogue with a partner about a relationship contract.

A relationship contract is an agreement, oral or written, to commit one's life and love to a partner—within a given time frame and set of parameters or guidelines—for the purpose of personal and relational growth, while protecting the emotional fidelity of the relationship. This chapter and the next will provide help for you and your partner in making conscious choices about what you mutually want your relationship to look like at this time.

Understand that such contracts are dynamic and need to change with the ebb and flow of any relationship. The model you had in mind at the beginning of your relationship may not work now. And the model you create now might not work one year, or five years, from now. The saying "When you have both feet planted firmly on the ground you are stuck" applies to relationships, as well. Relationships are constantly in flux, and trying to keep them looking the same year after year often leads to boredom, sexual disconnection and resentment.

So, why do we enter into relationships in the first place? Certainly relationships are about love, companionship, sharing the good times, sharing the bad times and caring for one another. Sharing and caring are essential ingredients of relationship growth. You will recall from Chapter Two, that growth, both personal and interpersonal, is the primary purpose of a passionate partnership. Love is an energetic connection and energy is always moving. Growth cannot, and does not, happen without change and movement. Growth requires risk—often necessitating the transcendence of some of our personal insecurity. Recall that safety in a relationship comes from the continuing realization that you can take emotionally challenging risks with your partner and still come out okay.

An attachment to the one we love can be considered secure or insecure. The nature of this attachment originates in the dynamics of the parent-child relationship beginning in infancy. Our adult attachment style will likely mimic our mothers' (or female caretakers') attachment style with us as we were growing up and our brains were developing. "Secure" attachments allow adult partners to be independent, yet connected. "Dismissing insecure" attachments are characterized by an independence that excludes (dismisses) one's partner, often creating feelings of abandonment in the partner. "Preoccupied insecure" attachments are characterized by an anxious attachment to (preoccupation with) a partner—to the exclusion of independence, and can create feelings of engulfment in the partner. When insecure attachments lead to an excessive and/or obsessive need for security and stability, a state of stagnation can ensue with minimal potential for movement, change and growth.

RELATIONSHIP PARADIGMS AND CONTRACTS

Rich and fulfilling relationships are more often characterized by taking reasoned and balanced emotional risks, creating sufficient safety to maximize potential for movement, change and growth. Moving into the future of your relationship with curiosity, rather than solely seeking security, eliminates idealized expectations that frequently create disappointment. No matter which relationship paradigm you and your partner choose, thinking of your partnership as a grand experiment—an exciting exploration—rather than simply a space for security and stability brings with it creativity, dynamism and fun.

Over time, some men in relationships feel confined. The once-sought-after stability may create a sense of stagnation. The stagnation, without having a method or means to change the relationship paradigm, is reminiscent of the Soviet experiment. Lack of choice may feel stable, comfortable and easy, but it often leads to frustration, resentment and dissatisfaction. As such, the seemingly most secure and stable relationships frequently end with surprising abruptness as a trapped partner seeks freedom, change and choice. All too often, the sense of security and stability is a false sense of security and stability as change is an inescapable part of life and relationships. *Just the notion of having options gives people hope for growth and change.* But, at the same time, options complicate life, and they require conscious awareness, thoughtful introspection, emotional integrity and considered conclusions. In relationships, open, honest dialogue and compromise about choice and change are necessary. Ultimately partners must take responsibility for their commitment to mutually accepted decisions and guidelines with openness to revision as the relationship matures.

> *Just the notion of having options gives people hope for growth and change.*

A common challenge in relationships occurs when what feels like a trap for one partner feels perfectly fine for the other. Attempting to control or manipulate a partner to decrease the anxiety associated with insecure attachment is likely to create a greater sense of entrapment or engulfment. When people feel trapped, they instinctively look for an escape. For a relationship to thrive—and not merely survive—and to realize increasing intimacy, there must be choice, change and challenge. Flexibility and openness to new ideas, new experiences and new choices brings life and energy to a partnership. Thinking of your relationship as a journey and not a destination will open your heart and mind to new adventures and excitement. Do not be afraid of change, embrace it—after all, it is inevitable.

Risk and reward are not the same for every person or every couple. The challenge for you will be finding a *balance* that allows you to hold on to your comfort zone without getting so comfortable as to avoid change. This balance will be in flux all the time, so *dialogue with your partner must be ongoing to continue to move the energy of the relationship within the bounds of mutual safety.*

When partners are at different places with regard to a model or paradigm for the relationship, extensive dialogue is required. I like to remind couples that they are a *team* reaching out to one another to find solutions for mutual happiness. This is not about right or wrong. There is no right or wrong. This is about transcending the *shoulds* and having a meeting of hearts and minds.

...dialogue with your partner must be ongoing to continue to move the energy of the relationship within the bounds of mutual safety.

Questions to Ponder:

1. Do you think of heterosexual marriage as the standard to emulate for your relationship? Do you have a role model of gay relationships to emulate? If so, how has such thinking impacted your relationship both positively and negatively?

2. What does it mean to you to envision your relationship as a journey rather than a destination? How have you grown in your relationship? How about your partner?

3. Do you think of your relationship as stagnant or dynamic? Do you ever feel confined or even trapped in your relationship? Would you like to see more change and movement? How might that be accomplished? Dialogue with your partner about these difficult issues.

Exclusive or Open

There are two broad categories comprising the basic framework of male-to-male intimate relationships: the sexually exclusive and the sexually open. I will be providing you with much more information about the open relationship paradigm than the exclusive paradigm. My attention to the open model is not because I have a personal or professional preference for open relationships, it is simply because the exclusive relationship is based on a model most of us are very familiar with: heterosexual marriage. If the definition of exclusivity is the limiting of sexual connection to one's partner—as it is in an exclusive relationship—there is a whole lot less partner discussion necessary in establishing sexual guidelines. As well, because most of us in our society grow up believing that exclusivity is the ideal, I will need to take some time to explain the notion that there is no ideal paradigm. In my practice, I work to help gay men understand that—while the exclusive arrangement is great for many men—it is not for everyone, and it is okay to work out an open arrangement with your partner. Again, that does not mean I am advocating an open relationship for everyone, but I would like to help to expand your consciousness on the issue to help you formulate a workable model for your unique situation.

I often hear that open arrangements "don't work" and lead to the end of the primary relationship. I also hear many men say that they cannot be monogamous (exclusive).

Both statements are true. And both statements are false. How can both statements be both true and false? Remember that, earlier, I espoused the value of being okay with ambivalence. Ambiguity is the normal condition of human brain function.

Men can certainly be sexually exclusive with one partner. Limiting your sex life to your partner is a choice. It is no different from the vegetarian who decides to limit his diet to vegetables, even though he may enjoy eating meat now and again. He does so because he feels the benefits of the discipline outweigh any pleasure gained by eating meat. And men who choose to be sexually exclusive with one partner feel the benefits outweigh any pleasure gained by having "extracurricular" sex. On the other hand, limiting sexual encounters does mean restricting an enjoyable activity men are biologically driven to experience. To quote Ryan and Jetha from their book *Sex at Dawn*, "…for most men, sexual monogamy leads inexorably to monotony." If the desire to have outside sex is very strong and your current sexual desire for your partner is not, containing your drive has the potential to create resentment and frustration.

Many men end their relationships not long after opening them; this is true. But to blame the ending on the opening is often shortsighted and misdirected. When sex wanes in a relationship, as we've discussed in Chapter Two, it is most often either because of a failure to communicate or a shifting sexual template. Opening a relationship up to outside encounters often occurs without any discussion about the underlying issues that created the lost sexual interest. As well, many couples open their relationships without any real agreement or contract as to how this new opening is going to work. The ending of a relationship after opening is generally not about the opening; it is either about a relationship that has already ended or about an opening that does not have parameters to protect the emotional fidelity already existing in the partnership.

RELATIONSHIP PARADIGMS AND CONTRACTS

There are many benefits, as well as limitations, to whatever arrangement any given couple chooses. Exclusivity is uncomplicated in its design. As with any machine, the fewer moving parts there are, the less likely there will be need for repairs. Exclusive sexual relationships require constant work on the physical connection—unless a couple chooses celibacy—creating grist for increasing vulnerability and, hence, greater intimacy. Assuming the couple's trust in each other is well founded (i.e., no one is cheating), there is less potential for jealousy, and it would be nearly impossible to bring home a sexually transmitted disease. The downside of exclusivity is the lack of freedom to choose to be sexual with others, which limits the variety and exploration that many men desire. When there is a lack of sexual desire for one's partner, this downside is magnified by the relationship's absence of sexual activity.

Open sexual relationships provide freedom to choose to explore sex with different men. Openness can be tremendously liberating, and, with parameters, can be hugely satisfying and safe. Men with waning desire for their partners may find the experience of outside sex enhances their fantasy lives and actually improves the sexual connection with their partners. *Talking about having an open relationship and setting up guidelines is a particularly vulnerable process for a couple.* The dialogue itself, in combination with the freedom to choose, often creates greater physical intimacy for couples. The downside of an open relationship is the possibility of jealousy and sexually transmitted disease. As well, there is a chance that one member of the couple may fall in love with a sex partner, leading to the end of the primary relationship. These concerns are real, but can be minimized with a well-formulated open relationship contract.

Those who argue that an open relationship is more likely to lead to a break-up because of sexual infidelity often do not take into account the fact that many so-called exclusive

> ∽
> *Talking about having an open relationship and setting up guidelines is a particularly vulnerable process for a couple.*
> ∽

relationships are secretly open or unfaithful. The most common reason men have sex with other men is not because they are unhappy at home—it is because opportunity knocks. Taking advantage of such opportunities in the context of an exclusive relationship is simply living a lie. Many men in relationships with other men live this lie. Often there is even an unspoken underlying assumption that a partner will cheat from time to time. Creating an intimate relationship means being honest about what you genuinely want—and discussing that with your partner. An open relationship out in the open with parameters is, in my view, a more honest and intimate relationship than one that feigns exclusivity or avoids talking about sex in a full and complete manner.

I have had many clients tell me they secretly have had sexual encounters within an agreed-upon exclusive relationship. These men argue that what their partners don't know won't hurt them. They tell themselves it is better to lie than to disappoint, and they hope they do not get caught as the disillusionment might harm the integrity of their relationships. To which, I reply, "What integrity?"

The noted psychologist Lawrence Kohlberg wrote his doctoral dissertation in 1958 describing the stages of moral development. He was not promoting a particular set of moral standards, but, rather, he was providing guidelines for observing human behavioral interaction. He speaks about six stages of development. The first two stages (Level One) are typical of childhood. Children make decisions based upon (1) obedience and punishment (i.e., how might I avoid punishment and what can I get away with) and (2) self-interest (i.e., what's in it for me, I don't care what might be good for you or mutually acceptable). The second two stages (Level Two) are typical of adolescents and adults who make decisions based upon (3) conformity (i.e., am I adhering to social norms) and (4) authority (i.e., am I adhering to the law). The final two stages (Level Three) are driven by wisdom, and decisions are based upon (5) a social contract protecting the general welfare of the public at-large (i.e., is this in the interest of the common good) and (6) universal ethical principles founded in abstract reasoning where unjust laws are disobeyed and right action is founded on empathic response (i.e., putting yourself in another's emotional and situational context).

Ideally, sexual behavior in intimate relationships would be based upon Stage Six—empathically directed integrity— where mutual understanding and honest open dialogue result in compassionate compromise. Such an approach is incompatible with a Stage One "what can I get away with?" "how do I avoid punishment?" and "what's in it for me?" style of deception.

One of the professors in my PhD program offered up the following assessment: *"What all men want is an open relationship where they are open and their partner is exclusive to them."* A main advantage of an exclusive arrangement is a feeling of safety, knowing your partner will not be enticed to go off with someone else. Of course, this can be a false sense of security, particularly if there are unaddressed problems in the relationship. In my view, the best reason for entering an exclusive arrangement is for the purpose of building trust and intimacy without distraction, diversion or escape. Such a mutual decision is one made out of love. The deep love often feels more committed in an exclusive arrangement. Exclusivity creates a context of "no escape" from the conflict, tension and pain inherent in passionate connections. As such, continuous intimate dialogue and resolution become invaluable. Choosing exclusivity to avoid jealousy or the anxiety of insecure attachments, on the other hand, creates a possessiveness trap. *Trying to control the sexual desires or activities of a partner to enhance your own sense of security is not about love or intimacy, it is about fear.* Recall the discussion in Chapter Two regarding decisions made out of love, versus those made out of fear. The argument often used in a jealousy-based exclusive relationship is that asking a partner for an open

Ideally, sexual behavior in intimate relationships would be based upon... empathically directed integrity...

Trying to control the sexual desires or activities of a partner to enhance your own sense of security is not about love or intimacy, it is about fear.

relationship is selfish. However, I'm not sure why asking for an open arrangement is selfish but asking for an exclusive arrangement is not.

Jealousy comes from the fear that you may lose something you think you have. Jealousy is about ownership and possession. Jealousy is the main cause of partner abuse, and it is the primary cause of spousal murder throughout the world. Clearly, this exceedingly potent emotion is both human and universal. Jealousy rules our desire to control our partners' behaviors. It originates as a primitive tool for keeping couples together for the integrity of the family. Its intensity is inversely proportional to a person's self-confidence and self-esteem. The more you feel unworthy or uncertain of your partner's commitment to you, the greater the likelihood of jealous reactions. *The best response to jealousy is self-reflection.*

The best response to jealousy is self-reflection.

If you become jealous, ask yourself one or more of the following questions: What is it about me that I am not accepting? Why do I feel threatened? What hot buttons are being pushed based upon my childhood experiences or previous relationships? How do I ask for the reassurance I need to feel safe? How might I discuss these with my partner?

The worst response to jealousy is to rein in your partner, placing controls that create a sense of entrapment or engulfment. A trapped man is going to look for an escape.

Questions to Ponder:

1. What is the framework for your relationship? Have you and your partner discussed an open-versus-closed framework? How might you begin a conversation about your relationship paradigm?

2. Is jealousy a factor in your decision-making process about the nature of your relationship paradigm? If so, what makes you jealous? How might you better deal with jealous feelings?

3. What do you see as the positives and negatives of an exclusive relationship? What about an open relationship? Discuss your feelings with your partner.

Why Do Couples Choose a Sexually Exclusive Arrangement?

A primary reason for choosing an exclusive sexual arrangement is to protect the integrity of the relationship from the potential passion of a new sexual connection. When first meeting someone we find sexually desirable, there is often a burst of the neurotransmitters dopamine and norepinephrine. These brain chemicals can create strong allure, and, like a drug, can draw us into wanting more sex with the man who activated them. The danger in an open relationship is that a partner may find himself in a near-addictive situation wanting to repeat a sexual encounter with one particular person. This is a risk to the primary relationship because of the development of limerence. "Limerence" is defined as "an involuntary cognitive and emotional state of intense romantic desire." The intensity of this type of desire can pull a partner from a relationship. You may well have experienced limerence at the beginning of your current relationship. And, as you have probably experienced, it typically does not last. As such, you run the risk of leaving a loving partnership for the enticement of a passing passion. Exclusivity is, in part, a commitment to avoiding this potential problem.

As previously mentioned, exclusivity is also a wonderful way to create high levels of intimacy. The commitment creates a safe container for deep interpersonal exploration. When things get tough sexually, there is no escape or outlet, instead, the partners have to face each other and their underlying feelings. These highly vulnerable exchanges enhance intimacy. As well, without seeking variety of experience outside the relationship, the couple must use creativity and imagination to keep the sexual energy moving. There is also greater motivation to engage conflict, since doing so is necessary to keep the sexual connection alive and well.

For couples who do not, or cannot, engage in sex with one another, the exclusivity keeps the relationship safe from termination for the expressed purpose of having a sexual connection. There is—in exclusive relationships—an evaluation, hopefully through continuous dialogue, about the importance of sex compared to the integrity of the loving relationship. It is 100% okay to agree to have a loving relationship without a sexual connection—there may be cuddling and kissing, or absolutely no physical contact. *Whatever two people decide for themselves is their business and is to be respected.*

Finally, for men with children, exclusivity—as in a traditional marriage model—can provide minimal external distraction and risk for the safety and stability of the family unit.

> *Whatever two people decide for themselves is their business and is to be respected.*

Why Do Couples Choose a Sexually Open Arrangement?

A primary reason men choose to open a relationship to other sexual partners is waning or lack of sexual desire for their primary relationship partners. Reasons for desire problems were addressed in Chapter Two, and include a failure to engage in intimate conflict resolution and the possibility of a shifting sexual template. When we first meet a passionate partner, as previously explained, there is a flood of dopamine and norepinephrine—both of which stimulate the desire for continued sexual exploration. As we become attached to a partner, the amount of dopamine and norepinephrine in the brain level off, and the levels of

RELATIONSHIP PARADIGMS AND CONTRACTS

oxytocin and vasopressin increase. These latter two are the chemicals of romantic, emotional bonding and attachment. Because men still desire the sexual surge they find with other men, partners may agree to a more emotionally connected primary relationship (oxytocin and vasopressin mediated) while getting sexual gratification (dopamine and norepinephrine mediated) elsewhere. The reason open relationships are workable is that *emotional fidelity is not the same as sexual fidelity.* As we will examine in Chapter Eight, the emotional fidelity in a relationship can be protected with agreed-upon parameters, despite sexual openness.

> ～
> *...emotional fidelity is not the same as sexual fidelity.*
> ～

Some couples choose to open a relationship simply because they want to experience sex with a variety of men, or because they want a variety of sexual experience that is not of interest to their partners. For example, one man may enjoy a BDSM scene or want to explore a particular fetish that is of no interest—or is a turn off—to his partner. Or perhaps one partner has an interest in having sex with women (i.e., bisexuality). Rather than forgo the life experience altogether, an arrangement can be created to facilitate such explorations.

For couples dealing with medical issues which make sexual function difficult or impossible for one partner, giving the sexually able partner permission for outside sexual contact is a beautiful expression of love and compassion. The physically compromised men who allow for such sexual openness are strongly confident in the emotional fidelity of their relationships and appreciate the desire for sexual enjoyment and fulfillment in life.

Other couples choose to have an open arrangement because they live at a distance or travel a great deal for work. Rather than go without sex for weeks or months on end—and rather than lie about containing sexual activity through the separation intervals—a couple may contract to allow outside encounters at certain times and under certain circumstances. (Again, we will get into the details of constructing relationship agreements in the next chapter.)

Finally, some couples open their relationships to honor the trust and confidence they have in the emotional fidelity of their connection. By giving each other the option to explore sexually, there is a sense of freedom to choose without a sense of being trapped, confined, possessed, owned or controlled. For many men, the openness is not about sex but about a sense of independence, and actual encounters are decidedly limited. As well, for some men the outside encounters improve and encourage fantasy, which can be brought back into—and enhance—the primary sexual relationship.

Questions to Ponder:

1. Given the broad categories of exclusive-versus-open arrangements, are you and your partner living your preferred relationship paradigm? How might you and your partner have a dialogue about your preferences?

2. How would you evaluate the integrity of your behavior within the framework of your existing arrangement with your partner based on Kohlberg's stages of moral development? Do you feel a change is in order to create more integrity and empathy in your relationship? How might you open this up to discussion with your partner?

Distinct Structure Types for Exclusive and Open Arrangements

There is a fairly broad range of possible agreements under the umbrellas of "exclusive" and "open" relationships. In the next chapter we will discuss creating an actual contract with very specific parameters, but here we want to look at the various ways agreements might be structured.

The following is a list of the most common relationship contract types, with a brief explanation of each. Feel free to consider which type would best suite your relationship as you begin to think about creating your own unique contract. Always remember that *relationship agreements are not set in stone and will change over time with the maturing of your partnership.*

> ∽
>
> *...relationship agreements are not set in stone and will change over time with the maturing of your partnership.*
>
> ∽

Sexually Exclusive Contract Types

1. Oral contract—the couple chooses an *informal* arrangement, based on a mutual agreement to remain sexually exclusive. There may or may not be a ritual or ceremony, frequently created by the couple, in which they publicly or privately demonstrate their commitment to one another. The couple may or may not live together.

2. Written contract—the couple adopts a *formal* written agreement to include sexual exclusivity. There may or may not be a ritual or ceremony, frequently created by the couple, in which they publicly or privately demonstrate their commitment to one another. The couple may or may not live together.

3. Monogamy Contract—the couple agrees to enter into a *legally binding* marriage contract with an agreement to remain sexually exclusive. There may or may not be a public ceremony, but there is usually a ritual or ceremony associated with the legal rite of passage, frequently religiously, ethnically and/or traditionally based. Married couples, with few exceptions, choose to live together.

Sexually Open Contract Types

1. Oral contract—the couple chooses an *informal* arrangement based on mutual agreement to include an opening to sexual activity, in addition to—or separate from—any sex they may have together. The

agreement may (a) limit interaction to activity in each other's presence with one or more individuals, (b) limit interaction to separate activity with one or more other individuals, or (c) combine both (a) and (b). The agreement may have very general to very specific guidelines, and may or may not be designed to protect the emotional integrity of the relationship. There may or may not be a ritual or ceremony, frequently created by the couple, in which they publicly or privately demonstrate their commitment to one another. Partners in this category may or may not live together.

2. Written contract—the couple adopts a formal written agreement to include an opening to sexual activity, in addition to—or separate from—any sex they may have together. The agreement may (a) limit interaction to activity in each other's presence with one or more individuals, (b) limit interaction to separate activity with one or more other individuals, or (c) combine both (a) and (b). The agreement may have very general to very specific guidelines, and is usually designed to protect the emotional integrity of the relationship. There may or may not be a ritual or ceremony, usually created by the couple, in which they publicly or privately demonstrate their commitment to one another. Partners in this category may or may not live together.

3. Marriage Contract—the couple agrees to enter into a legally binding marriage contract with an agreement that includes an opening to sexual activity, in addition to—or separate from—any sex they may have together. The agreement may (a) limit interaction to activity in each other's presence with one or more individuals, (b) limit interaction to separate activity with one or more other individuals, or (c) combine both (a) and (b). The agreement may have very general to very specific guidelines, and is designed to protect the emotional integrity of the relationship. There may

or may not be a public ceremony, but there is usually a ritual or ceremony associated with the legal rite of passage—often a composite of traditional observances and contemporary vows. Married couples, with few exceptions, choose to live together.

Other Contract Types

1. Polygamy—in most countries this constitutes an illegal heterosexual marriage between multiple partners agreeing to remain sexually exclusive within the family unit. Usually polygamous arrangements involve one husband married to multiple wives. The husband generally has sexual openness with all of his wives, and the wives are sexually exclusive with their one husband. There is often written documentation, and a ritual or ceremony with each marriage which may or may not be public. Polygamists generally choose to live in one household.

2. Polyamory—three or more partners (heterosexual, homosexual, bisexual, men and/or women) usually living together, forming an intimate unit. There may or may not be a written agreement, and there may or may not be an exclusive sexual arrangement limiting encounters to the partnership. The contract is based on various levels of intimate connection between the partners who enjoy sharing love, time and space with one another.

Questions to Ponder:

1. What contract type do you and your partner currently share? Do you feel it is adequate and satisfactory? If not, how might you discuss making a change with your partner?

2. Have you and your partner considered legal marriage as an option? Did you ever consider being legally married and having an open relationship? How might

you begin to open a conversation with your partner about expanding possibilities for your relationship contract? (The next chapter will help further your initial dialogue with questions to ask yourself about formalizing an agreement.)

Chapter Eight

Developing Your Creative Relationship Agreement

Chuck and Alan, men in their 60s, came in to see me at the ten-year point in their relationship. Both semi-retired, intelligent and in good physical condition, this couple was still very sexually active, having penetrative sex with one another one to two times per week. Chuck was the more outgoing of the two; Alan was more content at home with a good book. Chuck had been having sex outside of the relationship without Alan's knowledge for many years, often frequenting the bathhouse, going to sex clubs or having casual encounters with friends. Through the grapevine, Alan found out about one of Chuck's escapades with a mutual friend, and Alan was having a tough time with the betrayal—and Chuck's extracurricular activity, in general. Chuck couldn't understand why Alan would be so upset, as they still had a great life and sex life together. Prior to this event, there had never been any real dialogue or agreement about outside sex. As such, Chuck figured playing was okay, but chose not to tell Alan so as not to unnecessarily upset him. Alan, on the other hand, figured Chuck had been exclusive because they had an active and seemingly fulfilling sex life together.

The dynamics of the relationship helped me to immediately conclude that there was a very good Imago match and a very good sexual template match for this couple. This meant that my work as their therapist was to help Chuck and Alan figure out each other's (and their own) hot buttons. Not surprisingly, Chuck came from a family where every aspect of his life had been scrutinized and parentally directed. He did not want to be told what to do and what not to do. He did not want his partner to be his parent. Alan, conversely, came from a family where he was always overlooked or passed over because his younger brother was more outgoing, athletic and good looking. Alan did not want to be replaced by someone—anyone—else. And, as such, this passionate pair simultaneously pushed each other's hot buttons.

Therapy with Chuck and Alan had three significant challenges. The first challenge was to help the couple learn to dialogue about their hot buttons. The second was to restore the trust lost to betrayal. And, third, there was the challenge of finding a compromise to form the foundation of a new relationship contract.

Many partners coming to therapy with sexual fidelity issues are not having sex with one another, and so sensate focus might be added as a step prior to setting up a relationship agreement. Chuck and Alan, however, had continued to have excellent sex—even after Alan learned of Chuck's outside activity. The first two challenges were met head-on as this couple was very much in love and truly wanted to make the relationship work. The third task was the toughest, as Chuck wanted an open relationship to keep him from feeling reined in, while Alan wanted an exclusive relationship to keep him from feeling left out.

The dynamic shown in Chuck and Alan's situation is exceedingly common in gay couples. As previously mentioned, *gay men often struggle with the tension between autonomy and intimacy and its corollary fear of being engulfed versus fear of being abandoned. It is common for men to want to feel independent even when in a loving relationship. As well, gay men frequently have a history of feeling left out or left behind, being rejected or being abandoned. This is a feeling they do not wish to repeat in their relationships.* A contract that manages these opposing dynamics can be difficult to create, so the process is worth examining as you develop your own relationship agreement with your partner. This chapter will guide you through relevant questions to help create mutual agreement toward a relationship contract that is workable and unique to you and your partner.

> ~
> **It is common for men to want to feel independent even when in a loving relationship.**
> ~

As we discussed in Chapter Seven, relationship agreements or contracts fall into two major categories: exclusive and open. All relationship contracts have some common elements which I will present to you in the form of questions to discuss with your partner. Most important in the process is to think of your agreement as dynamic and open to review and discussion on an ongoing basis. You may decide today that you would never want children, for example, and then, as you watch your nephews and nieces growing up, you may change your mind. *Be open to change; change is the way of growth.*

> ~
> **Be open to change; change is the way of growth.**
> ~

Any relationship contract is an agreement you create in the present moment to guide your relationship experiment until a mutual decision is made to make a change. I cannot possibly provide the total spectrum of possible terms and parameters you may wish to have in your unique agreement. Think of this chapter as a guide. Put your minds and hearts together to add new and different aspects to your contract as you live your unique lives together. You and your partner ultimately need to decide what is important enough to be included in your personal agreement. The key points are not to avoid talking through the tough stuff, and not to make assumptions about any matter you may have on your mind.

Questions for *All* Relationship Contracts

Begin your process by going through the questions presented here by yourself, taking note of your answers with pen and paper. After both you and your partner have had a chance to come up with your individual answers and perspectives, set a date to dialogue and, as you did in Chapter Three, create a supportive environment to include all of the elements of a loving dialogue.

Now, more than ever, it is essential to be honest with yourself and honest with your partner—*totally honest.* Have a full and complete discussion, and for each question formulate a mutually agreeable conclusion that can be expressed in no more than three sentences.

If you have a problem coming to closure on any given question, take a break or skip the question, and come back to it at another time. One of you might want to take the role of recorder to be verified by the other. Writing your agreements down as you proceed will allow you to go back when you are finished, to review, make changes and come to a final, mutually agreed-upon version of your unique contract.

1. What is the purpose of your relationship agreement? Every relationship agreement has a unique purpose or composite of purposes for each couple. Here are a few examples from which you may wish to mix and match and/or add your own:

    (a) To affirm our love for one another

    (b) To take our commitment to one another to the next level

    (c) To create a foundation for greater intimacy and growth

(d) To agree to shared values as a basis for our relationship

(e) To protect the emotional fidelity of our relationship

(f) To create a context for building our loving family

(g) To define parameters for self-discovery and mutual exploration

(h) To help establish legal and financial commitments to one another

(i) To expand upon our marriage vows

(j) To agree upon the nature of our sexual relationship

> *Every relationship agreement may be reviewed and changed by mutual agreement at any time.*

2. When does this agreement begin, and when will it be reviewed for renewal? *Every relationship agreement may be reviewed and changed by mutual agreement at any time.* However, if you don't set a date to go back over it, you may find it becomes outdated or "changed" through assumptions without honest dialogue about how certain aspects feel to you from time to time. When creating an initial agreement, the newness of the experiment may necessitate more frequent revision in the future. I'd advise that you sit down to "review and renew" in one, three or six months to start. If you find, after this shorter period, that the agreement is working with minimal need to change it, then go to one year. If there seem to be multiple changes necessary, then review it again at short intervals. Annual review, perhaps on your anniversary date, is a good way to be sure, on an ongoing basis, that you and your partner are still on the same page. I strongly recommend—particularly with open relationship agreements—that you commit to staying together in the relationship no matter what happens until the review and renew

date. While a time frame may be seemingly arbitrary, the commitment allows for difficult dialogue to work through challenges that arise using the contract as a guide. The result is greater intimacy and growth as you commit to deal with, and not run from, challenging times.

3. How are you defining the sexual relationship at this time? Look back at the sexually exclusive, open and other categories discussed in Chapter Seven to select the one that best defines your current arrangement or the one you are hoping to create with your partner.

4. If you are not married, do you plan to get married in the future? Do you want to set a time frame?

5. If you are not living together, do you plan to live together in the future? Do you want to set a time frame?

6. If you do not have children or pets, do you plan to have children or pets in the future? How might this happen (i.e., adoption)? Do you want to set a time frame?

7. What financial arrangements do you have for your relationship? Do you each have separate finances, checking accounts, savings, credit cards, etc., or do you have joint accounts—or a combination of separate and joint accounts? Do you see some change in the near future which you need to begin to dialogue about now?

8. What legal arrangements are necessary? Consider real estate holdings, wills, trusts, life insurance, powers of attorney, living wills, etc. I strongly recommend consultation with a gay-friendly attorney who can advise you and help you draw up any necessary documents. Realize that *the relationship agreement you are formulating here is not a legal contract but rather a loving guide to growth and intimacy for you and your partner.*

...the relationship agreement you are formulating here is not a legal contract but rather a loving guide to growth and intimacy for you and your partner.

9. To what degree is being openly gay and having an openly gay relationship shared with your family, friends and co-workers? If you are not open about your sexuality, do you foresee that changing?

10. Do you want to have a ceremony or ritual to privately or publicly declare your commitment to your partner? If so, do you want to plan a date at this time?

11. Do you need to address modes of communication and parameters for time shared with one another? Often these parameters naturally develop in relationships but sometimes they do not feel all that comfortable. In other words, how often—and by what means— do you want to communicate? Some people cannot be disturbed at work during the day. Some dislike email and text messages as a means of communicating feelings. And how much time alone do you need? Do you want to have separate vacations, weekends or days to yourself? Do you want to agree to time that you absolutely spend together, for example, at dinner time nightly? And do you want to set a regular time for intimacy, dating and being alone together?

12. How will you maintain intimacy and growth in the relationship? What will you do to be sure you are addressing the conflict, tension and pain as it arises? What roles will touch, affection, seduction, initiation and sex play in your relationship with one another? How and when will you communicate about your sexual relationship? What exercises (i.e., sensate focus), activities and experiences do you want to include as a regular part of your lives? What will be the limits of your sexual exploration with one another?

13. What will you do if there is a breach of your relationship agreement? Can you agree to dialogue and possibly rework and renew the agreement? Will you access professional help?

Getting back to the scenario we discussed earlier in the chapter, Chuck and Alan decided that the purpose of their relationship agreement was to minimize hitting each other's hot buttons by opening their relationship—and by including specific parameters to protect the emotional integrity of their partnership.

The couple decided it was most important to create guidelines so Chuck would feel a sense of independence, while Alan would feel a sense of inclusion. They were not looking for any sort of formal commitment ceremony or declaration of their union, and they felt, at their age, that children and marriage were not in the cards. The couple was already living together and open to everyone in their lives. They had already taken care of all the legal and financial matters keeping their finances separate but naming each other as primary beneficiaries of their estates.

Chuck and Alan felt that the manner in which they communicated was fine. However, the need to be totally truthful needed to become an important new priority if trust was to remain high within the framework of an open relationship. (This came about subsequent to doing some challenging work in therapy around betrayal and trust.) Their sex life together was still enjoyable, and the spontaneity of their intimate time did not seem to need adjustment. The couple decided to establish the start and renewal dates for their agreement only after all the parameters for the open arrangement were mutually agreed to and accepted.

For couples choosing an exclusive sexual arrangement, the above questions may be all that is fundamentally required for a working relationship contract. However, for couples such as Chuck and Alan—and others in open relationships—the aforementioned questions are just the beginning, as you'll see below.

Questions for *Open* Relationship Contracts

Creating parameters for an open relationship is a formidable task. The majority of the rest of this chapter will be dedicated to helping couples find a way to be sexually open, while maintaining the emotional integrity of their relationships. Please note several critical points:

1. The best way to minimize risk in a sexually open relationship is by setting mutually agreed-upon parameters to protect the emotional integrity of the relationship.

2. Emotional fidelity is not the same as sexual fidelity, but extracurricular sexual relations can create limerence (strong desires) leading to relationship problems. Agreed-upon limitations that decrease this risk constitute the essential critical elements of an open relationship agreement.

~

Sexual openness does not mean "dating."

~

3. *Sexual openness does not mean "dating."* If you want to remain in your current loving relationship, the basic assumption is that you are not looking for another relationship. If you are looking for another relationship, perhaps you truly do not want to be in your current relationship. As such, what you want is not solely sexual openness—what you want is a new partner. Be clear and honest as to your intent. Dating implies more than sex; it implies creating an intimate relationship. You cannot protect the emotional fidelity of your relationship if you do not protect yourself from emotional attachment such as that which develops when dating.

4. Creating an open relationship agreement takes more time and effort than developing an exclusive contract. As such, there are more pages of this chapter dedicated to formulating an open agreement. This in no way is

to be misconstrued as this author's preference for one relationship type over another. As I've stated before, I have ~~no preference for~~ —nor do I advocate—any particular type of sexual arrangement. I do believe couples who wish to have an open relationship deserve professional guidance. I hope to offer some level of assistance in this chapter. Unfortunately, because most psychotherapists so adamantly adhere to traditional belief systems, repudiating sexually open relationships for being detrimental, there is little access to counseling for couples looking for creative solutions to sexual openness. However, as Ryan and Jetha affirm in their book, "Despite what most mainstream therapists claim...*couples with 'open marriages' generally rate their overall satisfaction (with both their relationship and with life in general) significantly higher than those in conventional marriages do.*"

> *"...couples with 'open marriages' generally rate their overall satisfaction (with both their relationship and with life in general) significantly higher than those in conventional marriages do."*

5. The more complex the agreement, the more likely it is to be misunderstood and/or violated—and the more closely and frequently it needs to be reviewed and renewed. When formulating guidelines, attempt to agree to the simplest arrangement that satisfies both partners' concerns.

6. If you and your partner are planning on sexual activity with others in each other's presence, there are specific questions to address later in the chapter. However, the following questions will guide *all* open relationship agreements whether the interactions are only in each other's presence, separate from one another, or both.

7. Again, before discussing this as a couple, go through each question on your own, writing down your sense of what would be best for you. You may also contemplate how your partner might feel, and to what degree you could accommodate him without compromising your own values or strong feelings. When you are both

prepared, make a date to dialogue, create a supportive environment and use the essential elements of a loving dialogue as you did in Chapter Three. Creating this contract is a process, and will likely take many hours of discussion. Plan to answer a few questions during each date to dialogue, and stop when you're at an impasse or feel tired. Do not continue if tempers rise or you seem to be going around and around on a particular issue. In my clinical practice, taking clients through these questions can take months to accomplish. Take your time to do it right—and respect yourself, your partner and your process.

Open relationship agreements work best with the following *four stipulations* clearly enumerated in the contract:

1. The partners agree to a start date—as well as a review and renew date—for the agreement, and the couple further agrees to stay together in the partnership no matter what happens with the open relationship experiment during that time frame. When challenges arise, the couple is encouraged to dialogue and make adjustments to the agreement rather than running from their commitment to one another.

2. The partners agree never to share personal or private matters about each other or the nature of their relationship with outside sexual contacts. Extracurricular sex is for the expressed purpose of exploring *sexual* adventure, and the sex buddy has no need to know that your partner is a brain surgeon and you have an open relationship because he's lost sexual interest in you. Leave your personal and private lives at home to protect the integrity of your partner and your relationship.

3. The partners agree always to practice safer sex as defined and agreed to by the couple. I would

recommend consulting your physician or other health professionals about risks and guidelines. At a minimum, it is critical to use latex protection for *all* anal penetration. *It is imperative that you include in your agreement specific terms regarding how you intend to protect yourself and your partner against HIV infection, or re-infection, and other sexually transmitted diseases and infections (STDIs).*

4. The partners agree that if there is ever a breach of safer sex practices as agreed to in the contract—whether intentional or not—*or* if there is a condom accident or other possible exchange of semen or blood that could put a partner at risk for HIV infection or re-infection or another STDI, there will be an *immediate* discussion and assessment of the situation. If either partner is concerned or believes there is any reason for concern immediate professional help will be sought.

The rest is up to you. Here are the questions to consider, discuss and find compromise around:

1. Now that you are agreeing to a sexually open arrangement, if you are continuing to have sex with your partner, what safer sex practices will you use with one another? Be sure to have a dialogue about the potential risks to your health in an open arrangement.

2. What type of open relationship contract do you and your partner wish to create? Will it include (a) limiting interaction to activity in each other's presence with one or more individuals, (b) limiting interaction to separate activity without your partner present, or (c) a combination of having sex with others both with your partner present as well as separately without your partner? Recall that your agreement is a time-limited experiment, and you may choose to change from one type to another after you test the waters. As you begin,

It is imperative that you include in your agreement specific terms regarding how you intend to protect yourself and your partner against HIV infection, or re-infection, and other sexually transmitted diseases and infections (STDIs).

it is a good idea to discuss what feels right to you for your relationship at this time. (Specific guideline questions for couples who plan to play together with others will be presented later in this chapter.)

3. When is it acceptable—and when is it unacceptable—to engage in outside sexual encounters? The possible answers to this question range from being okay "once a year on my birthday" to being *not* okay "on my birthday." You'll need to think this through and come up with your own list, but frequently agreements include:

(a) It's okay/not okay whenever we're apart geographically. One partner may be frequently out-of-town on business or perhaps you take separate vacations. For some couples, that is the perfect time to play; for others it is too threatening to think a partner is playing at a distance.

(b) It's okay/not okay when one partner is unavailable and you want to have sex. Partners may have different work schedules that make being together difficult. Some see that as an opportunity for an encounter without disrupting the partners' time together. Others do not like the notion of a partner playing around while they are hard at work.

(c) It's okay/not okay on special agreed-upon occasions. As previously indicated, for some a birthday or holiday may be a permissible "gift;" for others it is a violation of the sanctity of the occasion. Some couples agree to a very specific list of calendar days when it is not permissible to have outside encounters.

(d) It's okay/not okay on vacations. Some couples like to go to gay meccas to enhance the

189

possibilities of having sexual encounters, and the time off from the usual routine includes time off from the usual sexual routine. Other couples want to be exclusive and intimate only with one another when free from the stresses and distractions of day-to-day life.

(e) It's okay/not okay at certain times of the day. It may be acceptable to have a sexual encounter after dinner but not "during the dinner hour" because a couple may feel that dinner time is an important time to be spent together nightly. Some couples insist that a partner return home by a given time if he is out and about—for example, agreeing to always be home by 11:00 on weeknights and midnight on weekends.

(f) It's okay/not okay on certain days of the week. Some couples limit outside encounters to weekends or Saturday nights out. If Friday night is date night with your partner, with the intention of increasing your intimate connection with one another, then Friday night might not be best for outside encounters.

(g) It's okay/not okay for an encounter to interfere with previously arranged plans or to leave a partner when engaged in a non-routine activity to go off to have an encounter.

(h) It's always permissible to have outside sexual encounters. For some couples, limits regarding when to have encounters are not necessary to feel safe.

(i) It is only okay to have an outside sexual activity after checking in with your partner. (We will more specifically address matters that need to be communicated before an encounter later in this process. For now, just determine if you feel you need to have all encounter times approved by your partner in advance.)

4. Where and how do you plan to meet other men for sexual encounters? Examples of frequently agreed-to meeting scenarios include:

(a) Chance encounters. Many couples will agree to extracurricular sex "if the situation arises." In other words, if your partner is at work and you're at the grocery store and you meet an interested man, there is the possibility of an encounter. If this is an allowable scenario, then the question becomes "Is it okay to plan a date to have sex with this man at a future time or must permissible chance encounters lead only to spontaneous sex?" The reason this is a weighty decision is that some men who are fine with a partner engaging in a chance encounter have a problem with a partner planning a sex date. The notion that a partner is anticipating sex with someone else can be difficult. And this qualifier recognizes that a sex date is not the same as a date. *A sex date is just that—a date, or appointment, to have sex.* A date implies activities, sometimes intimate, with or without sex, and, as previously explained, is more likely to result in emotional infidelity.

> ~
> *A sex date is just that—a date, or appointment, to have sex.*
> ~

(b) The bar. Gay bars have traditionally been the meeting place for friendship, dating and sex. Is it okay for your partner to go to the bar to find sex?

(c) The Internet. Quickly trumping the bar as the place to find sex, is it okay for your partner to use various dating and sex sites online? If so, do you want to limit the selection or the amount of time spent cruising these sites? Is it okay to use your mobile device or smartphone apps? Some sites and apps are more designed for sex, and others are more geared toward relationships. If setting up a profile on a site or app, you then must discuss with your partner what information and photographs can, and cannot, be put online. Is it necessary to include the fact that you have a partner and are only looking for no-strings-attached sex? Is it necessary to have your partner approve your profile? How do you balance privacy with a partner's desire to know what you're up to? These can be thorny issues, but must be discussed fully if you are going to use the Internet for hooking up.

(d) The bathhouse, sex clubs, sex parties, nudist events, gay cruises and other venues that lend themselves to sexual encounters. As discussed in Chapter Six, some couples find such venues a total turn-off and others are quite comfortable sharing an experience at these locales. Some men feel a bathhouse is a very good place for encounters because the almost-totally anonymous nature of the sex is less likely to threaten the emotional fidelity of the relationship.

(e) Social events. Some couples do a good bit of socializing within the gay community and, as such, meet many men with whom they may have the opportunity to have sex. To what degree, if any, do you want to limit meeting possible sex partners at these events? Is it okay to go together to an event (or any other venue) and leave separately because one or both partners have met another man for sex play? Is it okay to get contact information in the presence of your partner for a later sexual encounter?

5. Where is it permissible—or not permissible—to have sexual encounters with other men? Here are a few of the most frequently agreed-to parameters:

    (a) The bathhouse, sex parties, sex clubs, nudist events, gay cruises and other venues that invite sexual encounters. Perhaps, if you go on gay cruises, you may agree to sex anywhere on board the ship except your cabin and/or in your partner's presence.

    (b) A hotel or remote safe and legal meeting place.

    (c) A public space with auspicious safety and/or legality.

    (d) The sex partner's home.

    (e) Your home. Many men find this a violation of the sacred space of their relationship; others are fine with the idea as long as they are not home. You must also consider the issue of safety when bringing someone you do not know well into your living quarters.

    (f) Your bed. For most men this is not an acceptable place for engaging in sex with anyone other than their partners, or with their partners and other sex players (as in a threesome).

6. With whom is it permissible or not permissible to have a sexual encounter? Careful thought and discussion is necessary for this seemingly simple—but not so easily addressed—issue. Here are some of the questions you need to ask yourself:

    (a) Is it okay to have sex with someone either partner—or both partners—know(s)? For example, perhaps you both work out at the gym together and frequently say hi to a sexy guy you know only by sight. When one of you goes to the locker room, Mr. Sexy asks the other if he's interested in some fun sometime. Does that feel safe, as you know you will both continue to see Mr. Sexy at the gym? What if you and your partner see different dentists, and yours—a hot, partnered gay man—asks you if you'd like to meet sometime for sex? If your partner doesn't know the man but you do, is that okay? Would that feel emotionally threatening to your partner? What limits do you need to set with regard to "dual" relationships (i.e., knowing someone in one context and also having sex with him) to feel the emotional fidelity of the relationship is protected?

(b) Is it okay to have sex with someone who is partnered? Is it important for you to know if the person you are having sex with is in a relationship and if they have an honest, open relationship? Some people feel it is uncomfortable, morally or otherwise, to have sex with someone who is cheating on a partner when you and your partner are working hard to have an honest opening to outside encounters in your relationship.

(c) Perhaps politically incorrect—however relevant—does the sex, race, religion or ethnicity of the sex partner matter? Some gay men are threatened more at the notion of their partners having sex with a woman than another man. There may be the feeling that, as a man, they are unable to offer a partner what the woman is able to offer. If you are not Latino, but you know your partner is highly attracted to Latino men—and he has a sexual encounter with the hot Hispanic guy who just moved in up the block—will you feel particularly threatened?

(d) Is it permissible to have encounters with drug users, smokers and/or drinkers? Often we do not know whether a sex partner is using, but, if you are aware, does that matter? If you have sex with a smoker and your partner smells smoke on your clothes when you get home, is that a problem? If you are in recovery, do you or your partner feel threatened by the idea of being with someone who is drinking? And, of course, if you have sex with someone who is using methamphetamine or some other drug during sex, are you enabling their drugging behavior—and does that matter to you or your partner enough to create a limitation in your open relationship agreement?

(e) Is it okay to pay to have sex with an "escort" (prostitute) or to have a massage with a "happy ending"?

> *Frequency is a critical parameter to set to feel safe in an open relationship.*

7. How often is it permissible to have outside sexual encounters? *Frequency is a critical parameter to set to feel safe in an open relationship.* The limitation could conceivably be anything from once per day to once per year. The frequency parameter I've seen most often is once or twice per month. You may state, for example, "no more than four encounters per month," if you're limiting to approximately one per week. I suggest a weekly, monthly or annual non-accumulating number. In other words, if a couple decide extracurricular sex twice a month is okay, and one partner does not have any outside sex in a given month, that would not mean it would be permissible to have four encounters the next month.

8. How often is it permissible to have sex with the same man? Remember that the intent of the limitation guidelines is to protect the emotional fidelity in the relationship, reduce anxiety, and decrease the

likelihood of limerence. The more someone engages in sexual activity with a particular individual, the more likely an emotional attachment will develop. Many men are capable of having sex without much, if any, initial emotional investment. Repeated sexual encounters, however, can evoke strong feelings which, in turn, can deepen the sexual connection.

If you wish to assure no potential for emotional connection, then you must have an exclusive arrangement. Minimizing the risk of creating an emotional connection in an open scenario requires limitation to one encounter per sex partner. Many men find this unsatisfactory as the initial encounter may be spontaneous, brief, a bit awkward and/or more of a "getting to know you and what you like" experience. The second encounter is often more comfortable and allows for a more fulfilling sexual scene—including activities you may have missed, but desired, the first time around. I find most men choose to limit their encounters to two per sex partner. Of course, this is more risky than just one, but each couple must balance risk against benefit. There are other couples who have riskier limits—including having no limit at all. Whatever you decide is fine, just be aware of how the risk to the primary relationship increases with each encounter with any given outside sex partner.

> *If you wish to assure no potential for emotional connection, then you must have an exclusive arrangement.*

9. How much time is permissible to spend with each sexual encounter? Most men do not place a limit here beyond being home by a certain hour. However, some people do not feel comfortable knowing their partners are spending an entire afternoon, evening or day with other men. One couple I worked with set a five-hour limit from the time each left their home to the time of return. Risk of emotional involvement may increase with the longevity of the encounters.

10. Earlier, there was a discussion of dating which begs the question: if you are meeting someone for the first time, perhaps after chatting online, is it okay to have coffee, first, to check out this person in "3D"? After the sex, is it okay to sit around the guy's house and have a drink? If you are meeting for a second time, can you have a bite to eat before or after sex? Again, the underlying question to ask is how much risk you and your partner feel is at stake. Each couple is different and will have different parameters and guidelines.

11. To what degree is it okay to communicate with the outside sex partner both before and after the sex date? Some couples choose to limit phone calls, texts and emails to specifics about the sex date (i.e., time, place). Others feel less compelled to place limits. However, as with other repeated activities, the more communication there is after an initial meeting, the more likely it becomes that there will be the development of a connection beyond the sexual experience.

12. What physical contact is permissible and what is not permissible? What limits do you and your partner wish to establish for the actual outside sexual activity? For example:

    (a) Is kissing permissible? Some couples feel kissing is highly intimate and want kissing limited to the primary relationship. Other partners feel that without kissing there is little sexual arousal and no real sexual connection.

    (b) Is mutual masturbation permissible? Considered the most benign of sexual contacts and the most safe, most couples do not place limits on masturbation or frottage (rubbing against another).

    (c) Is oral sex permissible? Most open agreements

allow for fellatio. The safer sex question is whether a condom is necessary and whether it is permissible to have a sex partner ejaculate into the mouth. Some couples go so far as to permit ejaculation, but not the swallowing of semen. There are many schools of thought on the relative safety of such oral sex practices. I refer you to your physician for up-to-date guidelines, and caution that *oral sex is not risk free.*

> *...oral sex is not risk free.*

(d) Is anal sex permissible? It is common for men to set limits on anal sex. Considered by many to be the most intimate of sexual activities, some partners want all anal penetration limited to the sexual relationship of the couple. Other men feel sex without anal sex is simply not sex, and the only limit they will set is to use latex protection for all penetrative activity. Still others will accept penetrating but not being penetrated, perhaps because it is perceived to be safer to top or because it is perceived that the act of surrendering is more intimate than being on top. Also, the acceptance of "topping" over "bottoming" is often the cultural standard for several ethnic populations.

(e) Is rimming permissible? Rimming, or anal kissing, is also considered a very intimate activity—as well as one that runs the risk of disease transmission. Some couples feel this is not an activity to participate in with a relative stranger. Other men feel it is an integral part of their sexual repertoire.

(f) Is vaginal sex permissible? If your open relationship includes sex with women, will there be any limitations on cunnilingus or intercourse? For men who are bisexual or want to explore sex with women as a part of the sexual opening, limitations other than the use of latex protection for penetration could severely restrict the sexual exploration.

(g) Is paraphilic sex permissible? Recall from Chapter Six that paraphilic sex includes activities other than oral, anal and vaginal sex. Is it okay to get involved in BDSM, fetish sex, water sports (urine play), etc.? What's okay and what's not?

(h) Is it okay to photograph or video your outside sexual encounters? If so, is it permissible to share these with others and, if so, with whom?

13. What sort of discussion with your partner is necessary, if any, prior to having an outside sexual encounter?

14. What sort of discussion with your partner is necessary, if any, after having an outside sexual encounter?

The majority of time I spend with couples on open relationship contracting is in review of those last two important questions. Many men spend years in their relationships either having outside sex (and not talking about it honestly) or having unspoken, unrealized sexual desires. You now are opening frank dialogue, and these questions ask you to consider the important matter of how you will continue the discussion process at the time of actual activity. Here are a few examples you might consider as you make your decisions:

(a) "Don't ask, don't tell." This policy didn't work for the United States military, and I'm not crazy about how it works with open relationships, either. I will say, however, many couples feel that "don't ask, don't tell" is the best workable approach. They will argue that they don't actually want to know what their partners are up to as long as they come home every night and remain emotionally connected. My concern with this approach is that for some men "knowing but not knowing" is more uncomfortable than simply knowing. If you are going to be anxious with the knowledge that your partner is having outside encounters without your knowledge of who, what, when, where or how and, therefore, will be magnifying in your mind the frequency and intensity of his experiences, then "don't ask, don't tell" will not work for you. With this approach, the partners also have no reasonable way of verifying the extent to which the agreement is being used as a guide for sexual exploration.

"Don't ask, don't tell" puts up a block to complete honesty and openness, which may ultimately decrease intimacy between the partners. At the same time, open communication about your exploration has the benefit of creating reassurance. The emotional connection is validated knowing it is strong enough not only to have the openness but to share its benefits with one another. Sharing information is a risk, but has the potential reward of strengthening the relationship. And, finally, talking about the sex may create fodder for fantasy during sexual times with your partner.

(b) "Don't tell unless asked." Some couples feel they'd rather not be told about every encounter, but want to be able to ask when they are feeling a bit insecure and need reassurance. Such an arrangement allows for verification of the agreement, as well as open dialogue when it is needed or desired. Of course, complete

> *"Don't ask, don't tell" puts up a block to complete honesty and openness, which may ultimately decrease intimacy between the partners.*

and full honesty in any answer is expected. Some partners fear for an unending series of questions, and so each couple must explore the limits of questioning. In essence, what do you want to hear about, and what do you *not* want to hear about?

(c) "Tell, but don't ask." This can be an intensely frustrating approach, but some partners feel they want to share information only to the extent that they are comfortable, without being grilled by a partner. Again, this can work if your contract is specific as to what information you want and do not want to hear.

(d) Prior to an encounter, share information about where and when it will take place and how long you will be gone. This approach may or may not include a requirement to check in and/or ask permission if an encounter is okay at the given time. Knowing the whereabouts of your partner, especially if an encounter is anonymous, helps minimize concerns for safety. There is also the reassurance experienced upon your partner's return, knowing that your partner has had his fun but has, ultimately, returned to you.

(e) After the encounter, share enough information to assure that the parameters of the agreement were followed, that the encounter was safe, and that the partner is still in love. Included in this is a reassurance of the emotional fidelity in the relationship. Some partners want to know every last detail of an encounter, especially if it is to be shared as fantasy for their own sexual interaction. Other partners want no details. The extent to which this is comfortable for each partner needs to be explored and written into the agreement.

No matter how much or how little you agree to share before
or after an outside sexual encounter, *the most valuable
communication involves a reassurance that—no matter what
happens elsewhere—the primary relationship, the mutual love
and the life you share together is more important than some
extracurricular fun.* Be sure to let your partner know with
regularity that the emotional fidelity in your partnership
is being protected by the guidelines you have agreed to
follow while opening the relationship.

One more thing to remember is that your outside sexual
partner(s) has/have feelings and emotions, too. You
and your partner may wish to have a policy of letting
your sex dates know that you are partnered and that you
have limits—including some covering the frequency of
encounters—that you honor and respect. Doing so gives
the potential sex partner the option of bowing out before
he becomes emotionally connected to someone who is
unavailable. Be fair to your sex buddies, realizing they are
human just like you.

Couples who plan to play together with other people have
even more work to do. Note that all open relationships,
even if limited to threesomes, do well to set parameters
based on the aforementioned questions. Here are some
additional *questions to ponder:*

1. If you are planning to play with others together, do
    you want to limit the number of people you engage at
    one time? Do you want to play with other couples, in a
    situation better known as "swinging"? If you and your
    partner are new to playing with others, I recommend
    limiting your encounters to the two of you plus one
    other. When there are more than three people, pairing
    off tends to occur, and you no longer will be having sex
    "with your partner."

> *...the most valuable communication involves a reassurance that—no matter what happens elsewhere—the primary relationship, the mutual love and the life you share together is more important than some extracurricular fun.*

2. When bringing others into your sexual space, do you want to agree always to ask the potential sex partner, in advance, if he is sexually interested in both of you? It is not always easy to find someone who will find both of you near equally attractive, but if you don't ask about your potential sex partner's interests you may set yourself up for a scene where one of you is having sex and the other is observing. Watching your partner have sex can be great fun for some couples, but can be terribly upsetting for others. Think about saying to the potential sex partner, "We like to be sure our guest star has sexual interest in both of us. If not, it's best for us to pass on this opportunity."

3. When bringing others into your sexual space, do you agree to let the potential sex partner know in advance that you practice safer sex? Despite all the knowledge about the use of protection, there are still many men who want "bareback" sex. Finding this out once you are in the act is no fun for anyone. I suggest discussing condom use—as well as your boundaries and limits— prior to the encounter. Some couples also ask about HIV status. Please realize that men don't always disclose the truth and/or may not accurately know their current status.

4. Do you want to discuss what kind of sexual encounter you are expecting prior to taking in a sex partner for you to share? How might this limit your choices? If you are looking for a vanilla experience with your partner and another man, you will want to be sure the man you're eyeing is not looking for a BDSM experience. If you and your partner are both tops, you likely do not want to take home another top. Come to some broad conclusions with your partner regarding what sort of conversation about sex is necessary or not necessary prior to each encounter.

5. Do you want to have a word or phrase to signal

your partner when you are okay with bringing on a particular player? Perhaps you've met at a bar and decided that someone is interested in both of you, they agree to play safe, and they seem to be sexually compatible, how will you know your partner is okay with sealing the deal?

6. Once sex is underway, do you want to have a word or phrase to signal your partner when you've had enough? Sometimes an encounter may not be working for one of you, and you may wish to end the scene. Coming out and saying "I'm done" may not be easy. Having some other signal such as "this has been nice" lets your partner know you want to send your guest star home. I strongly suggest agreeing to a policy that, no matter how into the scene one partner may be, if the other says "it's over," then it's over. As well, *adopting a "no means no" stance with regard to any particular activity during an encounter that is not feeling right is an essential part of the safety net you need to have with threesomes.*

7. If your arrangement includes having additional sexual players—both with and without your partner present—is it okay to have sex together with someone that one of you previously has had sex with separately? Is it okay to have sex with someone separately, once you have had sex with that person and your partner in a threesome? You may feel that there is less risk to emotional fidelity if you are present during sex with outside players, and so it may be okay to bring someone into the relationship for sex that one partner has already been with sexually. I would still advise a limit on frequency, as it is not unusual for a pairing off to occur if one partner is preferred due to the fact that he has already had a "getting to know you" session with the other partner. Remember that your parameters are being set up to protect the emotional fidelity of your relationship.

...adopting a "no means no" stance with regard to any particular activity during an encounter that is not feeling right is an essential part of the safety net you need to have with threesomes.

8. Go back over the list of thirteen questions previously presented for open relationships and see which parameters need to be applied to the encounters you and your partner share with others. For example, you may wish to limit the type of sex you have with other men in the presence of your partner, such as no penetrative sex. You may wish to establish how, when and where you are going to meet other men. For example, "We can connect with guys online and meet them at a coffee shop before having sex." Attempt to think of anything that might cause you some anxiety, and have a complete dialogue with your partner about ways to set guidelines to minimize any angst.

9. Do you want to agree to a debriefing after each sexual encounter you share as a couple? Negative feelings may come up after an encounter, and may include feeling jealous, feeling left out, feeling bored, feeling angry, and feeling empty, to mention a few. Positive feelings may also come up, such as feeling gratitude for having your partner, feeling more connected to your partner, feeling more sexually aroused by your partner, feeling exhilarated by the experience, and feeling satisfied. Talking about your feelings and how to reduce the negative and maximize the positive the next time around creates vulnerability and greater closeness with your partner.

When I was working with Chuck and Alan, they realized that they enjoyed their sexual time together without adding other men to the mix, and so their agreement decision was to open the relationship to separate outside sexual contacts. It was easy to agree to keep their private matters private, use safer sex practices and keep an open dialogue about any safer sex or contract breaches. The couple chose to define safer sex as using latex protection for all anal penetration and to avoid oral sex that includes ejaculation into the mouth. They also found that they felt most comfortable using protection for their sex together to minimize any risk of exposure to HIV or STDIs as a result of having sex with other men. They did not feel it necessary to limit where either could meet a sex partner or could have the encounters, or what sort of sex they could have.

However, in order for Alan to feel safe he insisted that Chuck never have sex with men either of them knew, never have sex with the same man more than twice, and never create friendships or allow emotional connections to develop with his sex buddies. Chuck agreed to tell all of his sex partners that he was in a solid relationship, and that the encounters were to be strictly "no strings attached." Alan also insisted there be no dating behavior of any kind— including no coffee meetings before or after sex. Phone, text and email were to be limited to exchanging information for the sex date. The couple further agreed to no overnight stays and to always returning home by midnight. As well, the couple agreed they would never have sex with others in their home, they would always put their plans for together time and their relationship before any outside encounters, and that, if they went out together, they would always come home together.

Chuck would not have to ask permission for outside sex, but he would have to tell Alan when he was having sex, where he was going and approximately how long he'd be gone. This check-in helped Alan feel included in the plans— if not the experiences—and reduced concerns about Chuck's safety when encounters were to be anonymous. Chuck agreed simply to acknowledge the experience after any encounters and take whatever time necessary for Alan to feel reassured. Chuck agreed to honestly answer any questions about the encounters, and Alan agreed not to be overly inquisitive about the specifics regarding the sexual activity. It was clear from the discussion that Alan had no plans to have outside encounters, even though the agreement was as open for Alan as it was for Chuck. Their contract was really about giving Chuck some freedom to explore while keeping Alan feeling as included and as safe as possible. The couple agreed to try out the new agreement for three months and then review and renew.

Obviously, creating the agreement was a long and arduous process for the couple. Difficult feelings were explored and my professional guidance was a critical part of their success. If you find it too challenging or overwhelming to engage your partner in these matters, *I highly recommend working with an open-minded psychotherapist or clinical sexologist to assist you through the contracting process.*

> *I highly recommend working with an open-minded psychotherapist or clinical sexologist to assist you through the contracting process.*

Verification of Your Relationship Contract

Relationship contracts, whether exclusive or open, are based upon mutual trust. No relationship can work without trust. No relationship *contract* can work without trust. The question often arises: "How do I know if my partner is keeping his word?" Well, there is no way to know for sure. Hopefully, if you've come this far in this book and done the communication work recommended, then honesty has become a foundation principle for all of your efforts.

When there is a purposeful breach of your agreement it is reason for true concern. If you are serious enough about making your relationship work to go through the difficult process of coming to a contractual agreement, then you need to be serious enough to keep your word. Again, it is vital to get professional guidance if you and your partner cannot resolve any problems you are having with your agreement, if the agreement itself—or its implementation—has you wondering whether you want to be in the relationship, or if you or your partner is in breach of the contract.

Relationship Contracts and Ceremonies

I strongly recommend that a written contract include some sort of ritual or ceremony. An oral arrangement is better than none at all, but when you write down your intentions you have a hard copy to refer to with your partner to review your agreement. You can be fairly certain there will be tough times that require serious dialogue. Knowing you've made a commitment in writing tends to solidify and make the agreement more powerful—as well as more accessible in the future. When you see your contract in writing, you may find there are things that are misunderstood or don't genuinely feel right to you. You can then work with your partner to reword the document before implementation or re-implementation.

Rituals and ceremonies create a powerful moment in time to mark and remember the commitments you are making to yourself, your partner and your relationship. They represent a time to move from an old choice to a new one. Ceremonies help you acknowledge and express gratitude for the past, while opening up to and welcoming the future. Determine for yourselves how your written agreement fits into a ceremonial process and whether it will be public or private. Sometimes couples choose to have a public ceremony or marriage to openly acknowledge the loving commitment they are making to each other. The relationship agreement may be signed, witnessed by someone you love (or, perhaps, by the therapist who guided you through the process), and toasted privately, such as at a time preceding or following the public rite of passage. Even if you are just looking to mark the significance of your new agreement without fanfare, create a loving atmosphere for the experience. Perhaps have a romantic, candlelit dinner at home. Or maybe you wish to sign your agreement at a place of significance for you, such as a mountain retreat, the place you first met or

> *Rituals and ceremonies create a powerful moment in time to mark and remember the commitments you are making to yourself, your partner and your relationship.*

at a restaurant of meaning to your relationship. Making the event special does not mean having to spend a great deal of money or time. It just needs to be memorable for you and your partner.

Chuck and Alan worked several months in therapy to improve their communication skills with one another, address each other's hot buttons and create a relationship agreement. The fascinating, but not unusual, result was that as they made themselves more vulnerable with one another (as Alan explained his need to feel included, and as Chuck explained his need to have some freedom), and as they discussed ways to create safety in the context of sexual openness, the couple became closer and closer. By the end of therapy, their sex lives with one another became even more intense and more frequent (yes, men in their sixties can be extremely sexual), and Chuck seemed hardly interested in outside sexual outlets anymore. What Chuck, and many men with satisfactory sex lives at home, wanted more than outside sex was the sense that he was free to explore without feeling he had a partner-parent telling him what he could and could not do. While Alan would still prefer an exclusive arrangement, he came to better understand and accept Chuck's needs. Alan trusted Chuck's intentions enough to show his love through this open accommodation with workable parameters. (See Appendix Five for Chuck and Alan's Relationship Agreement and Appendix Six for the Agreement Addendum.)

Chapter Nine

Relationship Sabbatical: A Creative Solution for Mending or Ending

Y ou and your partner have taken a courageous journey through the pages of this book. The result of your work has, hopefully, created a more intimate connection for the two of you with a better understanding of how to communicate and effectively actualize creative intimacy. This is not to say that there may not still be ambivalence about your partnership. You may still feel, at times, that the relationship with your partner is not what you would like for your life. *Feelings of ambivalence are a part of the wax and wane of intimate connections.* I would encourage you to frequently engage your partner in dialogue around your ever-changing awareness. Work within the context of your relationship agreement, and don't be afraid to suggest changes as you and your partner grow and evolve.

> *Feelings of ambivalence are a part of the wax and wane of intimate connections.*

It is also possible that you have worked through the exercises and questions in this book and find yourself more confused than ever about your relationship. You may be feeling *more* ambivalent than before and feel like you have one foot out the door. You may have noticed there is so much conflict at this point in your partnership that intimate, sane dialogue is impossible. Perhaps there is so little "energy" between you and your partner that a certain apathy has set in. Or, you may even feel surer than ever that you are not with the right partner. If this is the case, the best advice I can give you is to seek professional help before you make any major decision—including a decision to end your relationship.

Traditionally, when we seek therapy to save a partnership, we are thinking that the relationship will either work or we will have to split. There is an alternative, or at least an interim solution, that works for many couples: the relationship sabbatical. Note here that "works" does not necessarily mean that it saves the relationship. "Works," in this case, means moving a couple to a conclusion that is best for both partners with the understanding that the love they share can be the basis of mutual respect and honor for any eventual outcome. As with everything we've talked about in this book, going into a relationship sabbatical with curiosity, rather than expectation, will create the most honest and authentic result.

The Relationship Sabbatical

So what exactly is a relationship sabbatical? Originally proposed by Dr. Cathleen Gray, *a relationship sabbatical is a structured time-out* which gives the partners an opportunity to explore an unsettled sense of self. It potentially lays the groundwork for a refreshed relationship renewal—or for a respectful relationship termination.

Dr. Gray explains that expectations for relationships have dramatically changed in the last fifty years. The advent of mass media, the Internet, ease of transportation and higher standards of living have expanded our consciousness about what it is possible to experience or to achieve in life. There has been a simultaneous change in the adult developmental process, including an internal struggle with intimacy versus autonomy. Many individuals seek to end a

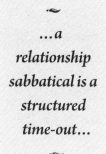

...a relationship sabbatical is a structured time-out...

relationship because there is an imbalance in this struggle within the context of the partnership. As we saw with Chuck and Alan, when there was more autonomy for Chuck, the intimacy in the relationship actually increased. But maybe an open relationship agreement is not the answer for you and your partner. Perhaps the autonomy question is about needing more time and space for self-discovery—sexually and otherwise—than an open contract affords.

The following situations might benefit from a sabbatical:

1. Your relationship is filled with extreme conflict, tension and pain. Time apart may provide a cooling-off period and an opportunity to see the conflict from a new perspective. (It is not unusual for arguments to be used as a means for gaining space, as a partner may retreat to the guest bedroom or the couch after an altercation.)

2. Your relationship is very low energy or you feel burned-out or bored in the relationship. Time apart may renew a sense of gratitude and passion for your partner. Expanded autonomy and a renewed sense of self have the potential to add new experiences and mystery to the mix of the relationship dynamics.

3. You are highly confused or ambivalent about your relationship. A sabbatical may give you time and space to gain perspective as to whether this is the right partner for you.

4. You've lost your sense of self. If you feel you simply don't know who you are anymore, a separation may be just what you need to rediscover your individuality, your interests and your true needs and desires.

5. You feel bad about yourself. Spending time working on your self-esteem may bring a new vitality to your partnership and help you to be sure that this partner is the one who brings out the best in you.

6. Your open relationship agreement does not afford you the autonomy you desire for sexual exploration. Working out a sabbatical arrangement with greater sexual freedom may help you establish a more workable open contract or help you understand what you honestly desire sexually.

Due to financial constraints, many couples looking to establish some space may try separate bedrooms, vacations apart or just "a night out with the boys" on a regular basis. Such solutions can be helpful to balance autonomy and intimacy, but for the situations described above they may be inadequate. As Dr. Gray would say, "some couples need to break the (relationship) contract in order to form a new, more functional relationship."

Important Note: If you and your partner have *any* legal, financial or relationship contracts with one another (i.e., own a home together, are married, have children, etc.) you *must* seek legal counsel prior to setting up a sabbatical arrangement. *The sabbatical may have legal implications that are different for each couple and for each jurisdiction.* This book offers suggestions for relationship exploration, only, and does not attempt to address any of the legal ramifications of a sabbatical.

The sabbatical may have legal implications…

You may be asking yourself, "Well, isn't a relationship sabbatical just a trial separation?" Indeed, it is a trial separation of sorts, but the sabbatical is structured and purposeful. As Dr. Gray explains, it includes a recipe, agreed to by the couple, for:

1. Breaking dysfunctional relationship patterns

2. Gaining perspective on the relationship

3. Realizing what your relationship and your partner actually mean to you

4. Creating a context for individual and personal growth and change

5. Finding a balance between autonomy and intimacy that works for you

The relationship sabbatical is a serious and unorthodox step with associated risks. It is quite possible that the time apart may create an awareness that your relationship is the most important aspect of your life, or it may help you to realize that you actually can live without your partner who is unable to meet your needs for a joyful life. There is no way to know at the outset how a sabbatical will unfold. As such, *it is highly recommended that your sabbatical be under the supervision of a therapist* who has experience with, or is open to, this approach.

> *...it is highly recommended that your sabbatical be under the supervision of a therapist...*

Elements of the Sabbatical

The sabbatical agreement, as with the relationship agreement, is set for a particular period of time. Unlike the relationship agreement, the sabbatical period needs to be *at least* three months, with six to twelve months as more beneficial lengths. A period of less than three months does not give adequate time for personal growth or perspective.

Any sabbatical period should *not* be a time of estrangement. It should be a time of engagement, albeit different from the standard interface of your current relationship. A couple taking a sabbatical should arrange the frequency of communication and meetings as well as the purpose of the communication and the meetings.

In addition, I recommend the couple see their relationship therapist weekly—at least in the initial phase of separation. Less frequent meetings may suffice after a time as directed by the therapist. The therapy can provide a safe environment for dealing with the feelings that arise during separation, individuation and changing perspectives. The therapeutic work also can help to maintain a couple's sense of connection with one another.

Remember, the sabbatical is *not* a divorce—even if it results in a break-up. The sabbatical should be a process of personal maturation resulting in relationship renewal, even if the terms of that relationship contract are altered dramatically. To that end, a sabbatical agreement also addresses living arrangements, financial considerations, personal goals and parameters for sex with others.

Questions to Guide Your Sabbatical Agreement

Run through these questions by yourself, first, as you did with the relationship agreement. Write up an agreement that would work for you. Anticipate your partner's feelings and how you might be willing to compromise in order to structure a workable arrangement for both of you. Then set a date to dialogue and create a supportive environment using the elements of loving dialogue as you've done in the past.

1. What will be the time frame for your sabbatical? Recall that three to twelve months is suggested for adequate growth and perspective.

2. Who will move out of your main residence (assuming you are living together)? This can often be the thorniest decision. There are financial implications attached to this decision, as well as emotional ones. If you and your partner agree to go forward with the sabbatical, you will need to address all aspects of your living arrangements, and any feelings about who will leave and who will stay. Sometimes, although

infrequently, both partners will move out, each to separate residences.

3. What financial arrangements or considerations need to be addressed? It is often difficult to maintain the same lifestyle when you are not living with a partner. Perhaps the more financially-able partner can help the less affluent partner through this period. How will you handle the mortgage, rent, taxes and other expenses you have been sharing?

4. What property and possessions will go with whom during this period? Clearly, if the sabbatical ends in divorce, there will be another go-round with this question later. For now, just determine who will keep what for the period of the sabbatical. This discussion will need to include any pets.

5. If children are involved, how will you deal with the temporary living arrangements and visitation? Again, if you have children, you *must* seek legal counsel on these matters.

6. What are your goals for personal growth through this period? You may envision yourself eating a healthier diet, working out more, taking classes, learning to dance or play golf, traveling, taking up a new hobby or writing a book. Create a plan—and plan to stick with it.

7. What do you plan to do during the sabbatical to make yourself a better partner—either to your current mate or to another in the future? Maybe you want to take some classes or workshops on relationships, join a self-esteem group, read books about making relationships work or get back in shape so you have more energy to share and enjoy. Note that self-improvement and personal growth activities, as per #6 above, also create better partners.

8. How often do you plan to meet with your therapist, both individually and with your partner? Plan for ~~weekly sessions~~ for at least the first month of the sabbatical, and work with your therapist on an appropriate timeframe thereafter.

9. How often do you plan to meet with your partner *outside of* therapy and for what purpose(s)? You may wish to have, for example, two meetings a week. Maybe you could have one right after therapy to process the session and the feelings you have about the sabbatical. The other meeting may be for lunch or dinner to discuss the business of your relationship, such as financial obligations or home repairs that need addressing. The key piece here is to make sure that your meetings have purpose.

10. How often do you plan to communicate during the sabbatical period? You may wish to limit phone, email and text messages by the day or week. Again, be sure your communication is purposeful and cordial, but not particularly social. It is easy to lean on one another at a time when being separate can be exceedingly tough. Remember that you are trying to gain perspective by exploring your autonomous self.

11. What social outlets will you explore? Do you want to reconnect with old friends and/or make new ones? Do you see yourself meeting people over the Internet, at the bar or at the gym? Will you join clubs or organizations where you may meet people with common interests?

12. What sexual contract do you wish to create with your partner? Do you want to go back through Chapter Eight and re-create a new open relationship agreement with parameters to be followed during the sabbatical period? Do you want a totally open arrangement with no formal guidelines? You must come to terms

with the fact that, without parameters, you run the risks discussed in Chapter Eight regarding limerence and getting emotionally involved with other men. Is that sort of openness for the term of the sabbatical going to be okay for both partners? How does autonomy and sexual exploration fulfill the purpose of your sabbatical?

After you and your partner have had a chance to sit down and hammer out a sabbatical arrangement, write out a contract as you may have done with the relationship agreement in Chapter Eight, sign your agreement, and have it witnessed by a trusted friend or the therapist that helped you through the process. (See Appendix Seven for a sample sabbatical agreement.)

I have found, in my practice, that couples tend to come to the conclusion—after careful consideration—that a sabbatical is a rather radical step as it approximates separation. As such, they would rather agree to work further on their partnerships within the framework of relationship agreements, find a way to lovingly end their relationships, surrender to the relationships as they are or just give up. Please note, "surrender" is not the same as giving up. *Surrender is accepting and embracing your relationship—and your life—with grace and gratitude. Giving up is resigning yourself to your life and relationship with despair and resentment.*

> *Surrender is accepting and embracing your relationship— and your life—with grace and gratitude. Giving up is resigning yourself to your life and relationship with despair and resentment.*

Those who are conflicted and/or in pain and choose to go into the sabbatical may find they achieve one of three results:

1. The attachment to their partners is too strong to live without them, and they often end the sabbatical before the term or the work is complete. The likely result is ending up back with the patterns they were struggling with before they agreed to the sabbatical.

2. There is a realization that their partners are not a good match and they choose to end the relationships. While this result might seem like a failure of the sabbatical experiment, couples usually have a much better understanding of themselves and the reasons they wished to end the partnerships. As well, there is often more mutuality of decision, as both partners have gained new perspectives on themselves and their relationship. Finally, because the couples have worked together on their feelings through the sabbatical process both in and out of therapy, the endings are generally more respectful, honest and loving with a true sense of closure and ability to move on.

3. The partners have rediscovered themselves and the reasons they were together with their mates in the first place. They reclaim their love for each other and realize that the relationship is important to them. The partners find new ways to balance autonomy and intimacy in their relationship, communicate for conflict resolution and re-contract to include matters of sexual intimacy, exclusivity and/or openness.

Whether a couple agrees to mend or end a relationship as a result of time apart, it is not unusual for a mutuality of decision to occur before the end of the sabbatical term. When both partners are sure and resolved, a mutual agreement to end the sabbatical can be discussed and determined with your therapist. Either choice necessitates continued therapy as a means to support a couple through either contract renewal or relationship closure.

Ending a Relationship

The bottom-line questions for anyone thinking about ending a relationship are, "Does my partner bring out the best in me?" and "Do I bring out the best in my partner?"

RELATIONSHIP SABBATICAL

I once heard a story of an eleven-year-old who was learning to play the clarinet in elementary school. He enjoyed the instrument and so his dad decided rather than rent a clarinet every year from the school he would buy his son an instrument of his own. They looked online for a used clarinet and went to the home of the seller. The seller had purchased a beautiful instrument for his daughter, who gave up playing when she went off to college. The young boy picked up the clarinet to give it a try, and both he and his father were amazed at the beauty of the tone coming forth from the instrument, compared to the one he was renting. They just looked at each other, having no idea that the boy could play so well. Simply put, to create beautiful music he needed the right instrument.

The same is true of relationships. To create beautiful music you need the right partner. Are you creating beautiful music with your partner?

This is a difficult question to answer honestly when there are considerable challenges in a relationship. But you likely know in your heart, after doing the hard work as presented in this book, whether you honestly want to stay in your relationship. As Daphne Rose Kingma explains in her book *Coming Apart: Why Relationships End and How to Live Through the Ending of Yours*, relationships serve a purpose for each of the partners, and when that purpose is complete for one or the other partner, the relationship is indeed over. I would say that *when the relationship realizes no further growth for one or the other partner the relationship is complete*. Some experts in the field truly feel that staying together—no matter what—is the only way to realize full intimacy. I believe these are questions best answered by individuals on their individual paths. If you feel your music would sound better with another instrument, then you are probably living with one foot out the door. I'm not sure that's fair for you *or* your partner.

> ...when the relationship realizes no further growth for one or the other partner the relationship is complete.

There may come a time when the pain which would be endured to stay in a relationship is greater than the pain which would be endured to end a relationship. If that time comes, the answer should become clear. Unfortunately, because it is often easier to end a relationship with anger and blame than with love and self-reflection, many choose to dig up all the hurt and pain of the past. There may be a tendency to focus on all the so-called negative characteristics of a partner to justify leaving a relationship. But, the fact is, at one time you loved this man you are now choosing to leave, and there were many reasons you held on and worked on the relationship.

This is not a time to brutalize your partner or beat up on yourself. This is the time to honor what you've had and respect your partner for who he is *and was* to you. If ever there is a time for a date to dialogue using all of the communication skills you learned in Chapter Three of this book, it is when you are considering ending a relationship. Direct your thoughts and discussions on your feelings and take responsibility for them. Blaming your partner will not create closure. Work with a therapist to review the process you went through with your partner.

Use the elements of a loving dialogue to create a new path and a new contract with your partner. Perhaps you'd like to find a way to be friends or confidants. If you've been together for a long time, this man may well have become your closest family member. Talk about how you might continue that sort of connection. It may take time to come to a place of comfort in your new way of being together. For some couples, that means absolutely no contact for a while.

The importance of discussing these matters cannot be overstated. Do not leave each other hanging. Dialogue about your feelings, the type of relationship you'd like to ultimately have with one another, and a projected path or plan for the immediate future. You may well have to discuss legal and financial matters. Do so with respect, dignity and fairness. Know that creating unnecessary legal or financial drama simply prolongs the pain and hurt, keeps you essentially tied into the relationship you claim to want to end, and prevents you from moving forward with your life. Seek legal counsel from a gay-friendly attorney who is more focused on reconciliation than remuneration. Get family and friends to support you emotionally through the difficult adjustment period. Work with a therapist on the tough feelings. Grieving the loss of a relationship may bring up memories and feelings of past losses.

> *Don't let others tell you when you should be done grieving.*

Give yourself time to find yourself anew. Don't rush the process. *Don't let others tell you when you should be done grieving.* People deal with loss differently. Be good to yourself. Know that the result of all the hard work you've done with your partner as you traversed the journey set forth in this book has created greater self-awareness and has prepared you for the potential of a more fulfilling and intimate relationship in the future.

On Being Single

Many men remain in difficult or unhappy relationships because of the fear associated with being single and starting all over again. Such thinking is validated by well-meaning people in good relationships who want to see their single friends happy and try hard to play matchmaker or vociferously profess the virtues of relationships. Others, in not-so-good relationships, may advocate staying in a bad relationship because they want to validate their own decisions to stay with partnerships that are not working.

I've even heard it said that it is better to be in a bad gay relationship than to be single, because single people are unhappy. Well, I've seen a whole lot of unhappy partners over the years, as well as many couples that put up a good show for the world but behind closed doors are quite miserable. *Coupling does not produce happiness in and of itself. Single men are not inherently unhappy, but being unhappy is not a good state of mind—or a good reason—for going into a relationship.* And, of course, many unhappy men remain single simply because other men don't want to partner with unhappy men.

First and foremost the man new to single life should work on making himself happy. If you decide to end your relationship, take the time to discover and explore your passions. Create purpose beyond finding a partner. Work on your sense of self, your confidence and your self-esteem. Being single can be an adventure and an opportunity to learn more about yourself, as well as learning what you want and what you don't want from life and from a partner.

As you date men, use the tools you learned from this book to develop intimate and honest dialogue. Before jumping into a new relationship, ask yourself what sort of Imago match and Sexual Template match are going on for you. Is there a passionate connection? Determine if there is a strong intellectual, emotional and sexual connection and expression. Ask yourself if you are falling into the same pattern(s) you did with your previous partner(s). This new time as a single man is a time of extraordinary potential. And, if you decide you wish to remain single, don't let the pressure of well-meaning friends, relatives and/or the culture push you into a life you do not want or are not ready to pursue. This is your life, and you have the right to live it as you see fit with dignity and self-respect. Enjoy!

> *Coupling does not produce happiness in and of itself. Single men are not inherently unhappy, but being unhappy is not a good state of mind— or a good reason—for going into a relationship.*

Questions to Ponder:

1. Do you ever feel you are living in your relationship with one foot out the door? How often have you felt strong ambivalence? Has it come and gone with circumstances over the years or has it been consistent? How does this impact your thinking about the longevity of your partnership? Would a sabbatical be of help? Why or why not?

2. If you and your partner are considering a sabbatical, what do you see as the potentially positive and negative aspects of such an arrangement? Could you formulate a draft of your own sabbatical agreement? What would the contract look like and how do you anticipate it would differ from your partner's proposal? Where might you find compromise?

3. Do you feel you and your partner bring out the best in one another? The worst? Are you creating beautiful music with the instrument you are playing? If not, is there still opportunity for relationship renewal? Can you surrender to things as they are, or is the pain associated with being in the relationship greater than the pain of letting it go? How do you discuss your feelings with your partner?

4. If, after doing the hard work presented in this book, you still have strong ambivalence, do you feel it is better to stay in your relationship despite sustained ambivalence in order to avoid hurting your partner or breaking your commitment? Or, do you feel the sustained ambivalence hurts your partner more in the long run? Under what circumstances is it okay to break a relationship commitment? Have you discussed these with your partner?

5. If you have been considering an ending for your relationship, what has stopped you? What are your fears and concerns for your partner? What are your fears and concerns for yourself? Does the thought of being single scare you or excite you? What are your feelings about living as a single man versus being partnered?

AFTERWORD

The Creative Process Continues

My partner, Charles, and I spent nearly two years in therapy. It was helpful to talk about our feelings, but it seemed like we went around and around and never moved forward with our sexual intimacy. Charles repeatedly asked the therapist for exercises, or something we could do to move the energy of our relationship forward. Those tools were never forthcoming. There was never any sensate focus, never any understanding of the role of our sexual templates and never any talk of relationship options. We finally did attempt a trial separation, which led to the ending of the relationship as there was inadequate guidance on how to creatively construct a sabbatical process. It was an extremely painful time for both of us.

Charles passed away, suddenly and unexpectedly, during the editing of this book for publication. I am so grateful that we stayed in therapy for six months after our separation. It gave us a platform to establish the close friendship we shared until his death. I look back and recall how, at the time we separated, I felt our relationship had failed. But, in actuality, it was a tremendous success. Despite our "break-up," our relationship continued in a more honest and authentic way. In many ways the intimacy of our connection was stronger after we moved apart. We found honesty in our ability to accept that we did not have, and could not work out, a sexual connection. But we could share a deep and abiding friendship and love without being in a partnership. To this day, Charles is the great love of my life, and I love him most for unconditionally loving me and letting me be me.

Charles read this book as it was being written, and he was excited about the potential it has for helping other gay men who struggle in their relationships. We talked about whether this book—or a therapist versed in the sorts of exercises, questions and relationship options presented in it—could have "saved" our partnership. Of course, we never came up with a definitive answer. However, we both agreed that had we had access to the processes you have experienced by reading this book, there would have been much greater likelihood that we could have worked through our challenges. To this day I consider Charles family, and I honor and appreciate the honest and respectful connection we worked to create.

If you came to this book to work on your own relationship, I hope that it proved a useful tool for you and your partner in navigating the complexities of your own creative intimacy. If you are a professional using this book as a reference to help gay men with their intimacy challenges, I hope you find the work as rewarding as I have for my patients. I would like to invite my academic and research sexology colleagues to use the qualitative material presented in this book to formulate quantitative methods, as further study is necessary for the rather unchartered territory of gay male intimacy. If you'd like to be in touch with me, feel free to contact me at *DrLeight@MarriageCounselingForMen.org*, or visit my web site at *www.MarriageCounselingForMen. org/SexHappens*.

APPENDIX ONE

Evolution of a Relationship

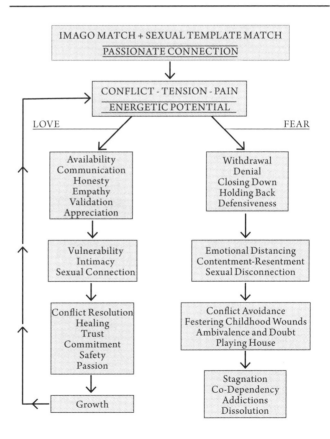

IMAGO MATCH + SEXUAL TEMPLATE MATCH
PASSIONATE CONNECTION

CONFLICT - TENSION - PAIN
ENERGETIC POTENTIAL

LOVE   FEAR

Availability
Communication
Honesty
Empathy
Validation
Appreciation

Withdrawal
Denial
Closing Down
Holding Back
Defensiveness

Vulnerability
Intimacy
Sexual Connection

Emotional Distancing
Contentment-Resentment
Sexual Disconnection

Conflict Resolution
Healing
Trust
Commitment
Safety
Passion

Conflict Avoidance
Festering Childhood Wounds
Ambivalence and Doubt
Playing House

Growth

Stagnation
Co-Dependency
Addictions
Dissolution

229

APPENDIX TWO

Inventory of Feelings

The following are feeling words that can empower your communication dialogues. Using "I Messages" you would structure your statements: "I feel (a word from the Inventory of Feelings)..." without using the words "you" or "your" in the message. The words in bold are commonly used, and it is helpful to keep them in mind when engaging in creative intimacy conversations.

A	amused	awed	C
abandoned	**angry**	awesome	calm
absorbed	anguish	**awkward**	capable
accepting	anguished		captivated
adamant	animated	B	cared for
adequate	animosity	**bad**	centered
admiration	**annoyed**	baffled	certain
adored	antagonistic	bashful	chagrined
adventurous	**anxious**	beat	**challenged**
affected	apathetic	**beat-up**	charmed
affectionate	appalled	beautiful	cheated
afraid	appreciated	bereaved	cheerful
aggravated	appreciative	**betrayed**	close
aggressive	ardent	bewildered	cold
agitated	aroused	bitter	combative
agonized	**ashamed**	blessed	**comfortable**
alarmed	astonished	blissful	comforted
alive	astounded	bold	compassion(ate)
alienated	at ease	bored	competitive
alone	attracted	brave	**concerned**
amazed	attractive	**bullied**	condemned
ambivalent	awake	burdened	**confused**

231

Inventory of Feelings (continued)

consoled
conspicuous
contempt
content
contrite
controlled
courageous
cowardly
cranky
cross
cruel
crushed
culpable
curious
cynical

D
daring
dazed
dazzled
deceitful
defeated
defensive
degraded
dejected
delighted
dependent
depleted
depressed
deprived
desirous
despair
desperate
despicable
despised
despondent
destructive
detached
determined
devalued
devastated
devoted
different
diffident
diminished
disappointed
discombobulated
disconnected
discouraged

disgruntled
disgusted
disheartened
disillusioned
disinterested
dismayed
displeased
dissatisfied
distant
distraught
distressed
distrustful
disturbed
divided
dominated
doubtful
drawn to
dread
dull

E
eager
ecstatic
elated
embarrassed
empathetic
empowered
empty
enchanted
encouraged
energetic
enervated
engaged
engrossed
enraged
enthralled
enthusiastic
entranced
envious
esteemed
estranged
evil
exasperated
excited
exhausted
exhilarated
expectant
exuberant

F
fascinated
fatigued
fearful
fed-up
fidgety
flustered
foolish
forced
forlorn
fortunate
fragile
fragmented
frantic
free
frightened
frustrated
fulfilled
full
fuming
furious

G
giddy
glad
gleeful
gloomy
good
graceful
grateful
gratified
great
greedy
grieved
guarded
guilty
gullible

H
happy
hassled
hateful
heartbroken
heavenly
helpless
hesitant
high
homesick
honored

hopeful
hopeless
horrified
hostile
humiliated
hurt
hysterical

I
ignored
imposed upon
impressed
impulsive
incapable
incensed
indecisive
indifferent
ineffectual
infatuated
inferior
inflamed
infuriated
inhibited
injured
inquisitive
inspired
insulted
interested
intimidated
intrigued
irritated
isolated

J
jealous
jittery
joyous
jubilant
jumpy

K
kind
kinky

L
lazy
leery
left out
lethargic

liberated
lifeless
listless
lively
livid
lonely
longing
loss
lost
lousy
love
loved
loving
low
lucky
lustful

M
mad
manipulated
marginalized
maudlin
mean
melancholy
mellow
miserable
misgiving
mistrustful
mixed-up
moody
mortified
mournful
moved
mystical
mystified

N
naughty
needy
neglected
nervous
neutral
nonchalant
nostalgic
nosy
numb
nutty

O
obnoxious
obsessed
odd
offended
offensive
open
open hearted
opposed
optimistic
outraged
overjoyed
overwhelmed

P
pain(ed)
panic(ked)
paralyzed
pathetic
patient
peaceful
perplexed
persecuted
perturbed
pessimistic
petrified
pity
playful
pleasant
pleased
powerful
powerless
precarious
preoccupied
pressured
proactive
proud
provocative
provoked
put off
put upon
puzzled

Q
quarrelsome
quiet

R
rage(ful)

rapture
rattled
reassured
rebellious
receptive
refreshed
regretful
rejected
rejuvenated
relaxed
reliable
relieved
reluctant
remorse
remorseful
removed
resentful
reserved
resigned
respected
restless
reverent
rewarded
righteous

S
sad
sated
satisfied
scared
screwed up
secure
self-conscious
sensitive
serene
servile
settled
sexual
sexy
shaky
shocked
shut down
shut out
shy
silly
skeptical
small
smart
sneaky

solemn
sore
sorrowful
sorry
spellbound
spirited
spiteful
stable
startled
stifled
still
stimulated
stingy
strange
stressed out
strong
stuffed
stunned
stupefied
stupid
suffering
sulky
sullen
sure
surprised
suspicious
sympathetic

T
talkative
tearful
tempted
tenacious
tense
tentative
tenuous
terrible
terrified
thankful
threatened
thrilled
thwarted
tickled
timid
tired
tormented
tortured
touched
tragic

Inventory of Feelings (continued)

tranquil
trapped
troubled
trusting
turned off
turned on

U
ugly
unappreciated
unbelieving
uncertain
uncomfortable
understood
uneasy
unhappy
unimportant

uninterested
unique
unloved
unnerved
unpleasant
unpopular
unsafe
unsettled
unsure
unworthy
upset
useless

V
validated
vehement
vengeful

vibrant
victimized
violent
vital
vivacious
vulnerable

W
wanted
warm
wary
weak
weary
weepy
wicked
wistful
withdrawn

woeful
wonderful
worked up
worn out
worried
worthless
worthy
wronged

Y
yearning

Z
zealous

APPENDIX THREE

Dialogue Analysis from Chapter Three

In Chapter Three, Bobby and Charlie sat down for a date to dialogue. Let's look at how they met—or missed—important points in their communication.

Acknowledge readiness to talk

Bobby: Hey, Charlie, I'm ready for our talk. Do you feel ready to start?

Charlie: I guess.

"I" Message

Bobby: I'm feeling a little anxious.

Empathy, Compassion, Love, Reassurance

Charlie: Me, too. But I know we need to move into a better place with one another. I do love you, you know.

Love, Appreciation

Bobby: I love you, too, Charlie. And I appreciate your willingness to do this with me.

Appreciation

Charlie: Thank you. I appreciate you, and I want you to know that.

Setting the environment for the dialogue

Bobby: So have you thought about where we should talk?

235

Charlie:	I think the two big chairs in the den would work. Maybe we could move them so they face each other. Would that work for you?	
Bobby:	Perfect. I was thinking the same. I'd like to do a few candles and just have the lights on low in the room.	
Charlie:	That's fine. Music?	
Bobby:	Actually, I'd rather not. I'd like it to be really quiet, is that cool?	
Charlie:	Totally. I'll disconnect the phone. And we need to put away our cell phones.	
Bobby:	Done.	

The couple set up the room and each take a seat. They are facing one another.

Bobby:	Can we just hold hands for a couple of minutes?	*Love, Asking permission to touch*
Charlie:	Sure.	
Bobby:	When I look into your eyes I see pain.	*Empathy, Compassion, Looking into each other's eyes*
Charlie:	I guess I feel upset that we have been arguing so much. I want things to be better.	*"I" Message, Reassurance, Compassion*
Bobby:	Well, that's why we're doing this. So, this is good. I feel upset, too, but it's going to be all right.	*"I" Message, Validation, Reassurance, Empathy, Compassion*
Charlie:	Well, I think it would be good to talk first about our "hot buttons," don't you?	*Initiating dialogue*
Bobby:	Sure, we can do that. Who's going to go first?	
Charlie:	I will, if that's okay. I've really been giving this a lot of thought.	
Bobby:	Okay.	

Charlie: Well, Bobby, as you know, my parents were always very overprotective. They needed to know everything I was doing. I remember, one time, a friend's mother paid for me and my friend to go on a carnival ride. When I told my mom about it she told me to never accept anything from anyone or go anywhere with anyone without asking her first—even though this was a friend who lived across the street, and our mothers were friends. My dad always would want me to go out and play ball with him, but I had no interest. So I realized, when I did that hot button exercise, that what I needed and wanted the most was to be allowed to choose to be with my own friends and do my own thing without being constantly watched and warned by my parents. And my last partner, Jim, was always on my case about where I was going and who I was with. I felt smothered and felt like he didn't trust me.

Mirroring

Bobby: So let me make sure I've got it. When you were a kid your parents were overprotective and didn't let you choose your friends or your own interests. And, with Jim, you felt smothered and that he didn't trust you.

Identify Hot Buttons

Charlie: Exactly. And so when you get upset about my going out with Tom it sets me off because it's like you're my mother. And it reminds me of Jim and how we ended things because of a lack of trust.

Empathy, Validation, Reassurance, Compassion

Bobby: Oh, wow, well that makes sense. I trust you…totally. And I want you to have your friends and do your own thing.

237

Charlie: Thank you.	*Appreciation*
Bobby: But I'd also like to come home after a hard day's work and find you home.	*Honesty*
Charlie: Well, I'm not your puppy dog. I need my freedom.	*"You" Message*
Bobby: I didn't say you were. Now here we go. I can feel myself starting to get angry.	*Defensive response*
Charlie: Me, too. Me, too. Okay, I'm sorry about the "puppy dog" comment. We need to find a way to compromise about this issue. Why is it so important for me to be home when you get home if you trust me so much?	*Honesty*
Bobby: Well, maybe this is a good time to talk about *my* hot buttons. When I was a kid we had a lot of family get-togethers. All the guys would be into throwing a ball around or playing touch football, and all the girls would be sitting around cooking and gossiping about the neighbors or other friends. I felt very left out and ignored. I'd end up playing some game alone, or reading a book off on the sidelines. And, in school, I wasn't into sports so I was always on the sidelines there, too. I remember watching the other boys playing and feeling very alone. So, when I come home and you're not here, I feel very alone. And knowing you're with someone else, even though I know it's not sexual or anything, I still feel left out.	*Identify Hot Buttons*
Charlie: So, let me be sure I get this so I'm sure we're on the same page. Growing up, you felt alone and left out a lot, and so now when I'm not home you feel alone?	*Mirroring*

238

"I" Message	*Bobby:* Well, sorta. Let me see if I can make it a bit clearer. It's not that I feel alone. I feel left out when you're with someone else and I don't get to share that with you. I enjoy feeling connected… especially with you. So, when I come home, I like to feel that connection with you.
Honesty	*Charlie:* Bobby, I can't be with you all the time.
	Bobby: I didn't say you had to be with me all the time.
Mirroring	*Charlie:* You said you want me home when you get home, or you'll feel left out.
"I" Message, Empathy, Validation	*Bobby:* Okay, okay, let me try again. I feel left out when I'm not included in activities that people I love are doing. I know I can't be with you all the time, but I also don't want to feel left out and disconnected. I understand that you need to have some independent space. I think we just need to find some way to balance the needs you have with the ones I have and compromise, like you said before.
Identify Hot Buttons, "I" Message, Reassurance, Validation, Empathy, Compassion	*Charlie:* Bobby, I don't want you to feel left out or disconnected. I can understand why you're feeling that way because of how it was when you were a kid, and I feel bad about hitting your hot button there. I want to find a way to make you feel connected and still be able to have my own time.
"I" Message, Validation, Empathy, Compassion, Honesty	*Bobby:* Well, thank you. I feel bad about seeming so possessive and getting on you about being out with Tom. I know you don't mean to leave me out. What kind of solution do you think we can come to?

239

Charlie: Would you feel better if I told you when I was going out without you?

Bobby: I felt this pang of pain when I heard "going out without you." Of course, I'd prefer you be home when I get home. For some reason that is very important to me. At other times, it would be great if you'd just tell me.

"I" Message, "It's important to me" Statement, Honesty

Charlie: I feel a bit boxed in by having to always be home when you get home, but if it is really important to you I will try to do that. If I really can't be home then—or if I'm going to go out—I'll just let you know what I'm doing.

"I" Message, Honesty, Compromise

Bobby: May I ask a favor, then?

Charlie: Shoot.

Bobby: I feel really anxious asking this because I know it could push *your* hot button, but it's also pretty important to me. If you are going out with friends and you're not looking for a little space or time alone with them, could you invite me along? That would really help me to feel included, even if I don't go.

"I" Message, "It's important to me" Statement, Honesty, Compromise

Charlie: I'll try to do that, too. Now may I ask you to do something for me?

Compromise

Bobby: Okay?

Charlie: Thursday nights I like to go to happy hour with Tom. You usually come home during that time. I'd like to be able to have that one night out with my bud without feeling like I've done something wrong. I know it makes you feel left out, but I need a pal other than you to share private stuff with, you know? You know

Identify Hot Buttons, Compassion, Love, Honesty, Validation, Reassurance, Empathy, "It's important to me" Statement

it's not the same as talking with you—you're my lover and my best friend. But you're not my "bud," you know. You're the one I'm in love with and want to be with every night. Tom is just the friend who has known me longer than anyone else in my life, and my private time with him is very important to me.

Empathy, Validation, Compromise, Reassurance, Love, Compassion	Bobby:	I really get your need for private time with Tom, and I respect it. I think we've come to a good solution. I love you so much. I'm really glad we had this talk.
Love, Honesty, Reassurance	Charlie:	Me, too. I love you, too, so much. I know we can make this work if we're honest with each other about our hot buttons.
Appreciation	Bobby:	Thank you for sharing your feelings with me.
Appreciation, Reassurance	Charlie:	You're the greatest!

APPENDIX FOUR

Effects of Angle of Entry on Rectal Insertion

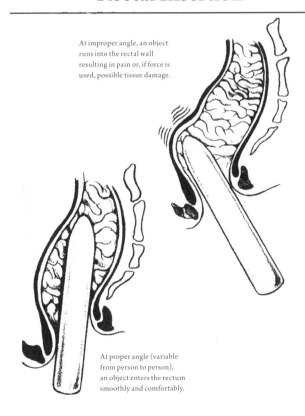

At improper angle, an object runs into the rectal wall resulting in pain or, if force is used, possible tissue damage.

At proper angle (variable from person to person), an object enters the rectum smoothly and comfortably.

Illustration from page 105 of *Anal Health and Pleasure*, revised 3rd Edition, ©1998 by Jack Morin, PhD

Example Relationship Agreement
(as created for Alan and Chuck)

This agreement between Alan and Chuck (also referred to here as the partners or the couple), commencing January 1, 2013, and terminating March 31, 2013, is created in love to allow us to explore outside sexual contacts within the stated parameters while protecting the integrity of the emotional fidelity of our relationship and honoring the commitment we have to one another.

Recognizing Chuck's need and desire for a sense of independence and Alan's need and desire for a sense of inclusion, we each agree to the following guidelines with the intent of being primarily sensitive to each other's needs and desires.

1. We are committed to our relationship with one another no matter what happens between us for the term of this agreement.

2. We are committed to continued work on our communication regarding needs for independence, inclusion, sexual freedom and sex with one another.

3. We are committed to continue to work on sexual intimacy with one another.

4. We agree to an open sexual relationship limited to encounters with other individuals, and separate from the sexual relationship we share together.

5. We agree never to share private matters regarding each other or our relationship, with any outside sex partner(s).

6. We agree always to practice safer sex, defined by us as using latex protection for all anal penetration and abstaining from oral sex that would include ejaculation into the mouth.

7. We agree to use the same safer sex practices with each other as described in point number six.

8. We agree to an immediate discussion and assessment of any breach of safer sex practices, whether intentional or not, and/or if there is a condom accident or other possible exchange of semen or blood. We agree to a medical consultation, should there be any doubt of exposure to HIV or any STDI.

9. We agree to no limitation on where it is permissible to meet outside sex partners, when the encounters can take place, the types of people who can be engaged or what sort of sexual activity can be involved.

10. We agree never to have sexual encounters with people who are known to either one, or both, of us.

11. We agree never to have sexual encounters with others in our home. All other locations are approved.

12. We agree to limit sex with any one individual to two encounters. We agree there will be no limit on the overall frequency of outside encounters.

13. We agree all outside sexual encounters will exclude any social interaction or dating, including, but not limited to, having coffee, a drink or other non-sexual meeting or interaction. We agree we will not create friendships or allow emotional connections to develop with any outside sex partner(s). We agree to limit phone calls, texts and emails to the details of meeting for sex.

14. We agree to prioritize our plans for together time and our relationship over any outside sexual activity.

15. We agree to no overnight encounters and agree always to be home by midnight.

16. We agree that if we go out together we will come home together.

17. We agree to disclose to all outside sex buddies—prior to any sexual activity—that we are in a relationship, that the meeting is to be a "no strings attached" encounter and that we have an agreement to limit sexual activity with any one person to two encounters.

18. We agree to a check-in prior to any outside sexual encounters, which will include disclosure of when and where the encounter is to take place and approximately how long it will last. If going to a bathhouse or sex club/party, the place and time will similarly be disclosed.

19. We agree to talk after any outside encounter, and to include acknowledgment of the experience and reassurance of our commitment to each other. Questions will be honored with honest and complete answers, but are to be limited with regard to a description of the sexual activity that took place.

20. We understand that any breach of this agreement—intentional or otherwise—requires immediate dialogue, review of the contract and its terms for renewal. Otherwise, the agreement may be changed at any time by mutual agreement. We, Alan and Chuck,

the partners, have read, discussed, agreed to, and commit to the above parameters based upon our love for and trust in, each other and our relationship.

Signature *(Alan)* _____

Date_____

Signature *(Chuck)* _____

Date_____

Signature *(Witness)* _____

Date_____

APPENDIX **SIX**

Example Addendum to the Relationship Agreement

(for Alan and Chuck) Found in Appendix Five

This addendum between Alan and Chuck is for the express purpose of extending our Relationship Agreement for the term April 1, 2013, through December 31, 2013. The agreement, as previously documented, shall remain unchanged. It is understood that changes can be made to the original document at any time by mutual agreement.

Signature *(Alan)* _____

                Date_____

Signature *(Chuck)* _____

                Date_____

Signature *(Witness)* _____

                Date_____

APPENDIX SEVEN

Example Sabbatical Agreement
(for Adam and Chris)

This agreement between Adam and Chris, commencing June 1, 2013, and terminating December 1, 2013, is created out of mutual respect for one another and the history of our relationship.

As there has been extreme conflict, we have come to the conclusion that time apart for the purpose of gaining a new perspective on the relationship and breaking dysfunctional patterns is necessary. We are committed to ongoing communication and personal maturation in order to come to a reasoned decision about the future of our relationship. We agree to these guidelines with the intent of being sensitive to each other's feelings and needs.

1. Adam will leave our joint residence within ten (10) days of the commencement of this agreement, and we will live apart for the duration of the agreement term.

2. Adam, being the more financially able partner, will continue to pay his share of the mortgage on the joint residence, and, at the same time, be fully responsible

for his own new residence. Adam will leave for Chris all furnishings and only remove from the joint residence his personal belongings. Chris will remain in the joint residence paying for his share of the mortgage, as well as the utilities, during the terms of the agreement.

3. Adam and Chris agree to see their couples' therapist once weekly, as well as seeing their individual therapists once weekly.

4. Adam and Chris agree to meet after their couples' therapy sessions for a minimum of one hour to discuss feelings that arise during the sessions.

5. Adam and Chris agree to meet one additional time every other week to discuss business matters related to their property.

6. Adam and Chris agree to attend an Imago weekend workshop together at some point during the first three (3) months of the sabbatical period.

7. Adam and Chris both agree to separately attend at least one eight- (8-) week group therapy session for gay men during the sabbatical period.

8. Adam agrees to take a class during the summer or fall semester at XXX University in the department of Black Studies and Chris agrees to take a class during the summer or fall semester at ZZZ Yeshiva University in Jewish studies as a means of personal growth, to better understand each other's backgrounds, and to otherwise potentially expand understanding and awareness.

9. Adam and Chris agree not to communicate outside of their therapy sessions, workshops or meeting times except in cases of emergency.

10. Adam and Chris agree to no sexual contact together, or with others, for the first three (3) months of this

agreement. After that time, a reassessment will be made to include parameters for openness, if necessary.

11. Adam and Chris agree to refrain from communicating in any negative way about each other with mutual friends and acquaintances. Social connections with friends and acquaintances may continue to occur but should not be entered into together as a couple.

12. Adam and Chris agree to reevaluate the relationship for re-contracting at the end of the sabbatical period. During the term of the agreement, a decision to end the relationship can be imposed, should either Adam or Chris decide it is no longer reasonable to continue the sabbatical experiment. Such a decision will be disclosed and processed in couples' therapy.

13. Adam and Chris understand this is not a legal document, and that all legal matters—including those with financial implications—will be agreed to in writing with the advice of legal counsel.

We, Adam and Chris, have read, discussed, agreed to, and commit to the above sabbatical terms and conditions.

Signature *(Adam)* _____

                        Date_____

Signature *(Chris)*_____

                        Date_____

Signature *(Witness)* _____

                        Date_____

REFERENCES

Introduction, "Intimacy is a...", Osho, *Intimacy: Trusting Oneself and the Other* (New York: St Martin's Griffin, 2001).

Introduction, "Intimacy requires...", Malone, Thomas Patrick, *The Art of Intimacy* (New York: Prentice Hall Press, 1987).

Chapter One, "There are an increasing number...", Green, Sonia, "Currency of Love: Customary International Law and Legalization/Recognition of Same-Sex Marriage in the United States," Paper presented at the annual meeting of The Law and Society Association, Renaissance Chicago Hotel, Chicago, May 2010.

Chapter One, "Homophobia can be defined...", Jacobson, Neil S. and Alan S. Gurman, *Clinical Handbook of Couple Therapy* (New York: The Guildford Press, 2002).

Chapter One, "Heterosexism, on the other hand...", Jacobson and Gurman, *Clinical Handbook of Couple Therapy*.

Chapter One, "He spoke of the persona...", Moacanin, Radmila, *The Essence of Jung's Psychology and Tibetan Buddhism* (Boston: Wisdom Publications, 2003).

Chapter One, "Growing up in a society...", Pachankis, John E., "The Use of Cognitive-Behavioral Therapy to Promote Authenticity," *Pragmatic Case Studies in Psychotherapy*, 2009.

Chapter One, "As such, gay identity development...", Jacobson and Gurman, *Clinical Handbook of Couple Therapy*.

Chapter One, "In his bestselling book…", Gray, John, *Men Are From Mars, Women Are From Venus* (New York: HarperCollins, 1992).

Chapter One, "It has been estimated…" Brady, Mark, "Why (many) Men (fathers) are Such Lousy Listeners," *The Committed Parent,* June 14, 2009.

Chapter One, "It is widely accepted…" Sanchez, Travis, et al, "Human Immunodeficiency Virus risk, Prevention and Testing Behaviors—United States," *National HIV Behavioral Surveillance System: Men Who Have Sex with Men November 2003—April 2005,* (Atlanta: CDC Surveillance Summaries, July 7, 2006).

Chapter One, "When you have an HIV test…", "HIV Infection: Detection, Counseling and Referral," last modified January 25, 2011, accessed September 17, 2012, *http://www.cdc.gov/std/treatment/2010/hiv.htr.*

Chapter One, "Additionally, tops…", "HIV Transmission," last modified March 25, 2010, accessed September 17, 2012, *http://www.cdc.gov/hiv/resources/qa/transmission.htm.*

Chapter One, "In a heterosexual relationship…", Ryan, Christopher and Cacilda Jetha, *Sex at Dawn: The Prehistoric Origins of Modern Sexuality* (New York: Harper Collins, 2010).

Chapter One, "According to PFLAG…", "Today's Gay Youth: The Ugly, Frightening Statistics," last modified 2010, accessed September 17, 2012, *http://www.pflagphoenix.org/education/youth_stats.html.*

Chapter One, "Methamphetamine brain damage recovery…", "Research Reports: Methamphetamine Abuse and Addiction," last modified September 2006, accessed September 17, 2012, *http://drugabuse.gov/publications/research-reports/methamphetamine-abuse-addiction/what-are-the-long-term-effects-methamphetamine-abuse.*

Chapter One, "Methamphetamine brain damage recovery…", Rosack, "Studies Show How Speed Exacts Toll on Brain," *Psychiatric News,* January 18, 2002.

Chapter One, "It is estimated…", "The Numbers Count," last modified June 26, 2008, accessed September 17, 2012, *http://wwwapps.nimh.nih.gov/health/publications/the-numbers-count-mental-disorders-in-America.shtml#Intro.*

Chapter Two, "The concept was originally conceived…", Money, John, *The Lovemap Guidebook: A Definitive Statement* (New York: The Continuum International Publishing Group, 1999).

Chapter Two, "The idea of a 'template' was coined and developed…", Granzig, William, "The Sexual Template and Erotology," Asia Pacific Conference of Sexology (Mumbai, India), November 23, 2004.

Chapter Two, "We cannot 'cure' our gay sexual orientation." "Just the Facts about Sexual Orientation and Youth," last modified June 2006, accessed September 17, 2012, *http://www. apa.org/pi/lgbt/resources/just-the-facts.aspx*.

Chapter Two, "The second force igniting sexual connections…", Hendrix, Harville, *Getting The Love You Want: A Guide for Couples* (New York: Harper and Row, 1988).

Chapter Two, "Exercise—Exploring Your Imago…", Hendrix, Harville and Helen LaKelly Hunt, *Getting The Love You Want Workbook* (New York: Atria Books, 2003).

Chapter Three, "Exercise One…", Hendrix and Hunt, *Getting The Love You Want Workbook*.

Chapter Three, "More information…" Nelson, Tammy, *Getting The Sex You Want* (Beverly: Quayside Publishing Group, 2008).

Chapter Four, "Sexologists are not in complete agreement…", Giugliano, John R., "Sexual Addiction: Diagnostic Problems," *International Journal of Mental Health and Addiction* (February 2009).

Chapter Four, "The APA has proposed…" Paris, Joel, *The Intellegent Clinician's Guide to the DSM-5* (New York: Oxford University Press, 2013).

Chapter Four, "Multiple factors are likely…", Kafka, Martin P., "Hypersexual Disorder: A Proposed Diagnosis for DSM-V."

Chapter Four, "As is the case with libido…", Morgentaler, Abraham, *Testosterone for Life* (New York: McGraw-Hill, 2009).

Chapter Four, "Erectile Disorder is…" Heidelbaugh, Joel J., "Management of Erectile Dysfunction," *American Family Physician* (February 2010).

Chapter Five, "Introduced in their book…", Masters, W. H. and V. E. Johnson, *Human Sexual Inadequacy* (Boston: Bantam Books, 1970).

Chapter Five, "In the 1980s Dagmar O'Connor…", O'Connor, *How to Make Love to the Same Person for the Rest of Your Life and Still Love It* (New York: Ballantine Books, 1987)

Chapter Five, "I wrote…", Leight, Arlen, *Sexual Enhancement Therapy for Gay Men in Long Term Relationships* (Miami: PhD Dissertation, 2004).

Chapter Five, "There are sexologists in the field…", Boyer, Bret A. and M. Indira Paharia, *Comprehensive Handbook of Clinical Health Psychology* (Hoboken: Wiley-Blackwell, 2007).

Chapter Five, "Paul Joannides, in his book…", Joannides, Paul, *Guide to Getting It On* (Oregon: Goofy Foot Press, 2004).

Chapter Five, "The rectum is not…", Morin, Jack, *Anal Pleasure and Health: A Guide for Men and Women* (San Francisco: Down There Press, 1998).

Chapter Five, "Much of the experience in this exercise…", Morin, *Anal Pleasure and Health: A Guide for Men and Women.*

Chapter Six, "This chapter includes…", O'Connor, *How to Make Love to the Same Person for the Rest of Your Life and Still Love It.*

Chapter Six, "Tantric sex was born…", Anand, Margo, *The Art of Sexual Ecstasy: The Path of Sacred Sexuality for Western Lovers* (New York: Putnam Publishing Group, 1989).

Chapter Seven, "Attachment to the one we love…", Wallin, David J., *Attachment in Psychotherapy* (New York: Guilford Press, 2007).

Chapter Seven, "To quote Ryan and Jetha…", Ryan and Jetha, *Sex at Dawn: The Prehistoric Origins of Modern Sexuality.*

Chapter Seven, "The noted psychologist Lawrence Kohlberg…", Puka, Bill, *Moral Development: A Compendium, Volume 3* (New York: Galland Publishing, 1994).

Chapter Seven, "Jealousy comes from the fear…", Marano, Hara Estroff, "Jealousy: Love's Destroyer," *Psychology Today* (July/August 2009).

Chapter Seven, "When first meeting someone…", Zeki, "The Neurobiology of Love," *FEBS Letters* (May 2007).

Chapter Seven, "When we first meet a passionate partner…", Zeki, "The Neurobiology of Love."

Chapter Eight, "However, as Ryan and Jetha affirm...", Ryan and Jetha, *Sex at Dawn: The Prehistoric Origins of Modern Sexuality.*

Chapter Nine, "Originally proposed by Dr. Cathleen Gray...", Gray, Cathleen, "Divorce or a Room of Your Own: Options for Troubled Marriages," *Family Therapy* (1995).

Chapter Nine, "As Daphne Rose Kingma explains...", Kingma, Daphne Rose, *Coming Apart: Why Relationships End and How to Live Through the Ending of Yours* (New York: Fawcett Crest Books, 1987).

INDEX

A

alcohol abuse
  as challenge in man-to-man relationship, 19–20
  inability to express feelings and, 20
anal penetration
  anal stimulation exercise, 121–128
  angle of entry for, 125–126, 243
  bottom or top sexual compatibility, 11–12
  clearing anal canal prior, 122
  defining top or bottom, 12–13
  massaging prostate, 124–125
  risk of HIV infection, 14–15
  safer sex practices, 16
  versatility and, 14
anal stimulation exercise, 121–128
appreciation, expansive communication and, 56–57
arousal, in sexual cycle, 36
attachment style, 160
autonomy, tension with intimacy challenge, 58

B

bathhouses, 148

BDSM, 150–151

bed-death phenomenon, 25

beliefs

about sex, 134–136

emotions and underlying, 44–45

bondage clubs, 150

bottom sexual role

defining, 12–13

explore anal stimulation exercise, 121–128

positions for pleasure exercise, 128–130

risk of HIV transmission and, 14–15

sexual compatibility issues, 11–12

C

cathexis, 25–26

ceremonies, relationship contracts and, 208–209

Coming Apart (Kingma), 221

communication of emotions, 41–78

appreciation, 56–57

compassion, 56

compromise, 57

date to dialogue, 62–64

determining your hot buttons, 46–64

dialogue analysis, 235– 241

empathy, 55

honesty, 57–58

hot button dialogue rehearsal exercise, 70–72

identifying elements of healthy dialogue exercise,
64–70

"I" statements, 54–55, 61, 73, 75

"it's important to me" statement, 61

love, 57

mirroring technique, 58–60

opposing hot buttons, 54

real thing exercise, 72–75

reassurance, 56

resolving your relationship conflict exercise, 75–78

underlying belief system and emotions, 44–45

validation, 55

"you" statement, 54

compassion, expansive communication and, 56

compromise, expansive communication and, 57

conflict, tension and pain

in relation to passion, 30, 32

resolving your relationship conflict exercise, 75–78

creative intimacy

characteristics of, xvi

defined, xv–xvi

cybersex, 152–154

D

date night, 138–142

date to dialogue, 62–64

deep-throating, 116

desire

declining or absent, 84–85

discussing, 36–37

disparity in level of, 81, 83

hypoactive sexual desire, 84–85

loss of, 73–74

in sexual cycle, 35–36

sexual template match, 36–37

dialogue. *See* communication of emotions

dialogue analysis, 235– 241

dismissing insecure attachment, 160

drug abuse, as challenge in man-to-man relationship, 19–21

E

electrosex, 151

emotions. *See also* communication of emotions

hot button pushed from missing need, 50

underlying belief system and, 44–45

empathy, expansive communication and, 55

erectile disorder, 86–88

causes of, 87
performance anxiety and, 87–88
treatment for, 87–88
erectile dysfunction, 86
exclusive relationship, 163–170
benefits of, 165, 167–168
contract questions for, 180–184
contracts for, 173
disadvantages of, 165
exclusivity defined, 158
intimacy and, 169–170
reasons couple choose, 169–170
exercises
determining your hot buttons, 46–64
explore anal stimulation, 121–128
exploring your Imago, 31
focus on touch, 94–105
hot button dialogue rehearsal, 70–72
identifying elements of healthy dialogue, 64–70
mapping your sexual template, 29
oral play and self-sex, 112–119
positions for pleasure, 128–131
real thing, 72–75
resolving your relationship conflict, 75–78
sensual responsiveness, 109–112
stimulation to orgasm, 119–121
touch and vulnerability, 105–109
explore anal stimulation exercise, 121–128

F
fantasy, to expand sexual experience, 142–144. *See also*
        sexual fun, frolic and fantasy
fear
in evolution of relationship, 32–34, 229
expressing feelings and, 32–33
as opposite of love, 33
feelings
fear of expressing, 32–33
inventory of, 231–234

men avoiding expressing, 10, 32

substance abuse and inability to express, 20

fellatio, 114–116

fetish, 150

fisting, 151

focus, performance anxiety as misdirection of, 87–88

focus on touch exercise, 94–105

G

gay identity development

as challenge in man-to-man relationship, 7–9

challenges of differences in, 7–9

Getting the Love You Want (Hendrix), 29, 50

Getting the Sex You Want (Nelson), 58

Granzig, William, 25

Gray, Cathleen, 212, 214

Gray, John, 9

Guide to Getting It On (Joannides), 114

Gurman, Alan S., 4

H

Hendrix, Harville, 29, 30, 33, 50

heterosexism, 4

HIV

anal penetration and risk of, 14–15

as challenge in man-to-man relationship, 15–18

knowing your HIV status, 15, 17

minimizing risk of transmission, 15, 16

regular testing, 17

safer sex practices, 16

homophobia, 4

homosexual, definition of, 26

honesty, expansive communication and, 57–58

Hopkins, Johns, 25

hot buttons

childhood memories, 46–47

determining your hot button exercise, 46–64

hot button dialogue rehearsal exercise, 70–72

opposing, 54

pushed button from missing need, 50

real thing exercise, 72–75

relationship memories, 48–49

hotel sex, 146–147

How To Make Love To The Same Person For The Rest Of Your Life And Still Love It (Dagmar), 91–92, 136

Human Sexual Inadequacy (Masters and Johnson), 91

Hunt, Helen LaKelly, 50

hypersexual disorder, 82

hypersexuality, 82–83

hypoactive sexual desire

diagnosing, 84

treating, 84–85

I

Imago

defined, 29

exploring your Imago exercise, 30

match, 30

impotence, 86

inhibited orgasm, 86

intimacy. *See also* sexual intimacy evolution/dissolution

defined, xv

exclusivity and, 169–170

honesty and transparency requirement, xv

tension with autonomy challenge, 58

vulnerability and, 33, 78

"I" statements, 54–55, 61

"it's important to me" statement, 61

J

Jacobson, Neil S., 4

jealousy, relationship paradigm and, 168–169

Jetha, Cacilda, 18, 164

Joannides, Paul, 114

Johnson, Virginia, 91

Jung, Carl, 5

K

Kingma, Daphne Rose, 221
Kohlberg, Lawrence, 166

L

Leather Universities, 151
limerence, 169
loss of desire, honest discussion about, 73–74
love
  expansive communication and, 57
  fear as opposite, 33
Love Map (Hopkins), 25

M

male character, temperament and personality, as
    challenge in man-to-man relationship, 9–11
man-to-man relationship challenges
  alcohol, substance abuse and mental health, 19–21
  anal penetration and sexual compatibility, 11–15
  gay identity development, 7–9
  HIV, 15–18
  intimacy and autonomy tension challenge, 58
  male character, temperament and personality, 9–11
  self-acceptance, 4–7
  testosterone, 18–19
marriage contract, 174–175
Masters, William, 91
Men Are From Mars, Women Are From Venus (Gray), 9
mental health, as challenge in man-to-man relationship,
    19–21
methamphetamine addiction, 20
mirroring technique, 58–60
Money, John, 25
monogamous relationship, 158. *See also* exclusive
    relationship
  defined, 16
  safer sex practices and, 16
monogamy contract, 173
moral development, 166–167

267

N

naughtiness factor, 138–139, 147, 149

Nelson, Tammy, 58

monophilic sexual activity, sexual template, 27

O

O'Connor, Dagmar, 91–92, 136

open relationship, 159, 163–168

  benefits of, 165

  contract example, 245–248

  contract questions, 180–207

  contracts types for, 173–175

  disadvantages of, 165

  reasons couple choose, 170–173

  stipulations for contract, 187–188

oral contracts, 173–174

oral play and self-sex exercise, 112–119

oral sex

  deep-throating, 116

  guidelines for, 114–116

  oral play exercise, 113–114

orgasm

  in sexual cycle, 36

  stimulation to orgasm exercise, 119–121

orgasmic disorder, 86

P

paraphilic sexual activity

  to expand sexual experience, 149–152

  sexual template and, 27

passion, conflict in relation to, 30, 32

performance anxiety

  as major cause of E.D., 87

  as misdirection of focus, 87–88

persona, 5

phone sex, 152–154

pornography, to expand sexual experience, 144–146

positions for pleasure exercise, 128–131

premature ejaculation, 86

preoccupied insecure attachment, 160

prostate, massaging, 124–125

public sex, 147–149

R

rapid ejaculation, 86

real thing exercise, 72–75

reassurance, expansive communication and, 56

relationship contracts

    defined, 159, 179

    dynamic nature of, 159–160

    example, 245–249

    exclusive, 173

    marriage contract, 174–175

    monogamy contract, 173

    open, 173–175, 245–248

    oral contract, 173–174

    questions for all contracts, 180–184

    questions for open contract, 185–207

    rituals and ceremonies, 208–209

    sabbatical agreement, 251–253

    verification of contract, 207

    written, 173, 174

relationship loop, 34–35, 229

relationship paradigm, 158–163

    defined, 158

    entrapment, 161–162

    exclusive relationship, 158–159, 163–170

    jealousy and, 168–169

    monogamy, 158

    open relationship, 163–168, 170–173

    stagnation, 161

relationships. *See also* exclusive relationship; man-to-man

    relationship challenges; open relationship

    attachment style, 160

    on being single, 223–225

    ending, 220–223

    evolution of, 31–35, 229

    passion and conflict in, 30, 32

relationship loop, 34–35, 229
   sabbatical from, 211–220
relationship sabbatical, 211–220
   defined, 212–213
   elements of, 215–216
   example agreement, 251–253
   purpose of, 214–215
   questions to guide agreement, 216–219
   results of, 219–220
   situations that benefit from, 213–214
resolution, in sexual cycle, 36
Ryan, Christopher, 18, 164

S
sabbatical, relationship. *See* relationship sabbatical
safer sex practices, 187–188
   minimum requirements for, 16
safety, from surviving emotional vulnerability, 34
secure attachment, 160
self-acceptance
   as challenge in man-to-man relationship, 4–7
   as essential precursor for intimate partnering, 5
self-sex exercise, 112–119
sensate focus, 91–92. *See also* sensual journey exercises
sensual journey exercises
   background for, 91–93
   explore anal stimulation, 121–128
   focus on touch, 94–105
   oral play and self-sex, 112–119
   positions for pleasure, 128–131
   sensual responsiveness, 109–112
   seven key guideposts, 112–113
   stimulation to orgasm, 119–121
   supportive elements for, 93
   ten important guidelines, 97
   touch and vulnerability, 105–109
sensual responsiveness exercise, 109–112
sex addiction/compulsion/hypersexual disorder
   disagreement over diagnosis of, 82

disparity of desire, 83

disruption or unmanageability of daily life, 83

Sex at Dawn: The Prehistoric Origins of Modern Sexuality (Ryan and Jetha), 18, 164

sex clubs, 148

Sexual Aversion Disorder, 85

sexual compatibility, man-to-man relationship challenges, 11–15

sexual cycle, 35–36

sexual desire. *See* desire

sexual disorders

erectile disorder, 86–88

hypoactive sexual desire, 84–85

orgasmic disorder, 86

sex addiction/compulsion/hypersexual disorder, 82–83

Sexual Aversion Disorder, 85

Sexual Enhancement Therapy for Gay Men in Long Term Relationships (Leight), 92

sexual fun, frolic and fantasy

BDSM, 150–151

cybersex or phone sex, 152–154

dating your partner, 138–142

examining sexual beliefs, 134–136

fetish, 150

fitness, 137

hotel sex, 146–147

naughtiness factor, 138–139, 147, 149

paraphilias, 149–152

pornography and paint, 144–146

public sex, 147–149

selfishness and, 137–138

sexual energy and, 136–137

sexual fantasy, 142–144

sexual shoulds, 134–135

tantric sex, 153

sexual intimacy evolution/dissolution, 23–40

bed-death phenomenon, 25

conflict resolution and, 30

discussing desire, 35–38
evolution of relationship, 31–35
fear of expressing feelings, 32–33
sexual template, 25 29
sustainable sexual intimacy, 38–40
vulnerability related to intimacy, 33–34
your Imago, 29–31
sexual shoulds, 134–135
sexual template
  age, 27
  body modifications, 26
  cathexis, 25–26
  changing nature of, 28
  defined, 25
  demeanor, 26–27
  desire and match in, 36
  mapping your sexual template exercise, 29
  match in, 28
  physical attributes, 26
shadow side, 5–6
singlehood, 223–225
stimulation to orgasm exercise, 119–121
substance abuse
  as challenge in man-to-man relationship, 20
  inability to express feelings and, 20

T
tantric sex, 153
testosterone, as challenge in man-to-man relationship,
    18–19
top sexual role
  defining, 12–13
  explore anal stimulation exercise, 121–128
  HIV risk for, 17
  positions for pleasure exercise, 128–130
  risk of HIV transmission and, 14–15
  sexual compatibility issues, 11–12
touch
  focus on touch exercise, 94–105

touch and vulnerability exercise, 105–109

V
vacuum aspirators, 87
validation, expansive communication and, 55
venous retention rings, 87
versatility in sexual roles, 14
vulnerability
   intimacy and, 33, 78
   touch and vulnerability exercise, 105–109

W
water sports, 150–151
women
   dealing with feelings, 9–10
   verbal abilities and, 10
written contracts, 173, 174

Y
"you" statement, 54

ABOUT THE AUTHOR

Arlen Keith Leight, Ph.D. is a diplomate of the American Board of Sexology, a board-certified clinical sexologist and licensed psychotherapist. He received his BA in psychology from The Johns Hopkins University, his MSW from The Catholic University of America, his psychodynamic psychotherapy training from The American University, and his PhD from Maimonides University. Dr. Leight is a Clinical Social Worker and Sex Therapist in private practice in Fort Lauderdale, Florida, and founder of One Broward Marriage Counseling for Men. Dr. Leight has written and lectured extensively on the topic of gay male intimacy, dating, human connections and relationships and has served on the faculty of several universities.